Remember When

By

Michael William Rhodes Ewen

Forward by Nancy Ewen

Edited by Joan Fleischer and Nancy Ewen
Cover Page Illustration by Lynn Lecoz
Chapter Symbol by William R. Ewen
Back Cover Illustration by Elizabeth M. Ewen

Order this book online at www.trafford.com
or email orders@trafford.com

Most Trafford titles are also available at major online book retailers.

Printed in Victoria, BC, Canada.

ISBN: 978-1-4269-3142-0 (sc)

ISBN: 978-1-4269-3143-7 (hc)

Library of Congress Control Number: 2010907091

Our mission is to efficiently provide the world's finest, most comprehensive book publishing service, enabling every author to experience success. To find out how to publish your book, your way, and have it available worldwide, visit us online at www.trafford.com

Trafford rev. 5/26/2010

www.trafford.com

North America & international
toll-free: 1 888 232 4444 (USA & Canada)
phone: 250 383 6864 • fax: 812 355 4082

Remember When

This book is dedicated to by beautiful wife Adriana and presented to her as a gift on our 20th wedding anniversary.

Forward

I am honoured to be given the opportunity to write a forward for this incredible piece of work. This chronicle is the product of many hours of thoughtful contemplation, worked from memory onto paper, read and re-read to ensure a perfect rendition of reminiscence. It was a privilege to have been trusted with the cherished memories, both innocent and intimate, of a couple I hold dear to my heart. The following pages include a history beautifully written in the words of a husband to his wife of those first times together. Although the memories are more than twenty years old, the words transform from the page into a vivid picture of a young couple coming together for the first time.

Michael's humour and good nature are vibrantly presented; his words describe the events as they happened from his point of view. I found the stories to be heartfelt and real. I could feel the coldness and sense the dread of those long, wet hours on the highway. I could sense the anticipation of coming together and the excitement of catching that first glimpse of a loved one stepping down from the bus. In particular, I felt the heartache of watching his loved one trapped in the undercarriage of the bus and falling to the ground, losing her grip on the cherished rose he had given her, only to discover that he had entered this section of the story as a joke to its editor: me. *

Reading Michael's memoir proves to me that my considerate and thoughtful older brother grew into an attentive, caring, and selfless husband and father. I have always been proud of his accomplishments and am further moved by the compassion and love he holds for his wife.

Nancy Ewen.

*** See appendix**

Preface

Dear Adriana,

You are my wife, my lifelong companion, and my best friend. My most cherished memories are the times that we have shared together. The first time I saw you, you were so beautiful. I can still see you walking towards me in your black leather miniskirt. You were stunning! I remember sharing a glass of wine with you that day. You bought a bottle of wine at the mall to celebrate your twentieth birthday. As we all sat around the table at Uncle Herman's house having a toast to you, I remember looking over at you. As you tipped your glass back, you closed your eyes. The oval curve of your closed eyes trimmed in long black eyelashes struck me as so beautiful and sexy. I have always admired the shape of your eyes. That evening we went to the movie theater with my cousins. We watched "Heart Break Hotel." I sat with Sanford, while you and Caroline sat behind us. All I could think about during the movie was how much I wanted to be sitting with you. Afterwards, the four of us were standing outside of the movie theater, and I made a point of standing beside you making small talk. I cannot remember what we were talking about; I just remember wanting to be near you. Later that evening, I was in Uncle Herman's basement talking with Sanford and his friend. You were upstairs visiting. Before you went home for the night, you came downstairs, looked through an opening in the doorway, and said goodbye. Your face was so beautiful. You were so happy and full of life. I remember thinking that your accent was so attractive and sexy. After you left, Sanford's friend commented on how cute you were. I went to sleep that night thinking about you – and I could not stop thinking about you over the next three months. I met you in October, and it took me until January to get the courage to ask you out on a date. The memories of that first day when I met you are dear to my heart. In so many ways, our first encounter was one of chance, and it frightens me to think of how close I came to not meeting you.

I will never forget our first date, when we held hands. We were at the movie theater when you reached over and took hold of my hand for the first time. You were the first girl that I ever took to the movies. As we sat in the darkness of the theater, you put your hand into my hand and our flesh touched. This is one of my most cherished memories. I think I must have held your hand for the rest of the evening. Afterwards, we went to Lou Lou's, and we danced. That was the first time that we kissed. I will never forget that kiss. We were dancing, and you kissed me, there on the dance floor. There must have been a thousand people around us, and I felt as if we were all alone. That is a memory that I will cherish for the rest of my life. You were so beautiful, and you were my date. After I kissed you goodnight for about ten minutes at the apartment building, I walked home, and thought about the evening. I thought about everything: meeting you at the bus station, our meal at the Chinese restaurant, the movie, dancing, holding your hand, and kissing you. As I walked home, I could not believe that I was on a date with such as beautiful girl. I was closer to you that night than I had ever been with anyone. It was the best night of my life and I did not want the evening to end. I was so scared that perhaps you would not want to see me again. I fell in love with you that night. All I knew was that I wanted to be with you as much as possible for the rest of my life. Twenty years later, I still feel the same, and I am more in love with you than ever. I cherish the memories of our first date. That was the night I first held your hand and our lips first touched. You made me feel so special! I was, and still am, so in love with you!

I will never forget the next day either. I was so happy when you called and wanted to spend the day with me. We met at the Town Square Mall. We kissed again, as we stood outside of the mall in a cool winter rain. I was hoping that we would kiss again. Until you kissed me I was afraid that perhaps you were having second thoughts. When you kissed me as we took shelter from the rain, it felt so good to be close with you, and to know that you still wanted to be with me. On the taxi ride back to my apartment, we held hands in the backseat. I remember moving my thumb around to feel your hand. It felt so good to have your hand in my hand. We went back to my apartment and we watched two movies. I cannot remember what the movies we watched were about. I only remember being so happy that you were with me. I was even happier when John McDonald decided not to watch the second movie, and left us alone. We lay on the couch and kissed some more. I felt so good embracing and kissing you. I could not believe that such a beautiful girl wanted to be with me. I did not want the weekend to end – I wanted it to last the rest of my life. Until that weekend, I never knew what it felt like to be truly happy and to feel like I truly belonged with someone.

There are so many more memories I have with you, and I cherish them all. The time I first brought you home to meet my family, the time you gave me my Valentine's present on the train and the conductor found us kissing in the narrow corridor, the time you came to my apartment for the week when I finished my third year, and especially that evening after our motorcycle ride to Orangeville. Remember the day we met in March? You came to Waterloo to surprise me, and we met on the street. I remember looking up, and was so happy to see you walking towards me. You were stunningly beautiful in your black leather miniskirt, long black nylons and a white lace trimmed top. You looked incredible!!! We spent the afternoon in the Bombshelter. Then there was the day I bought my futon bed, and you helped me carry it home, because I was too cheap to take a taxi. I remember the first day you took me to Toronto for a visit. I remember being nervous with so many people around and not knowing my way around the city. I put my wallet in my front pocket and stayed close to you. I think that you knew I was a little nervous. These are but a few of the wonderful memories of us that I cherish.

Marrying you was the best thing that ever happened to me. You have given me two beautiful children, and twenty years as my lover, my companion, and my best friend. Over the years, I have come to love so many things about you and our relationship. I love when you lay your head on my shoulder as we sleep, and when our feet touch in bed. I have always found your feet so sexy. I love your Romanian accent, the warmth of your eyes, and how I feel when we are together. I treasure our gentle intimacy, our erotic passion, watching movies with you Friday evenings, and the closeness we share in the darkness of the night.

I remember our first year of marriage. We have come so far from our one room pink apartment. We only had a single size futon bed, and an old bed frame as a stand for our twelve inch black and white television. I remember walking with you on Sundays and going to the movies on Tuesday nights. I remember one evening, walking hand-in-hand back to our small apartment from the theater, as it lightly snowed. I think that we watched Edward Scissor Hands that evening. We didn't have much back then, but we had each other. The only transportation we had was our motorbike. I used to love riding with you. You would often put your arms around me and give me a little squeeze. I used to love it when you did that. Remember the day we were riding in the rain and we took shelter under a highway overpass until the rain stopped? As cold and wet as we were that day, it was still so nice sitting there with you in our leather jackets as we leaned into each other's body for comfort and warmth watching the cars go by. Today when I see a young couple on a motorbike, it brings back fond memories of you and me when we were young.

I warmly remember the evening of January 2, 1996, when we sat in the dimly lit Red Dog Inn Restaurant after a long day on the highway. There was Frank Sinatra music playing in the background. In the faint candlelight of the restaurant you had such a special glow about you. I could not stop staring at you, as I thought about how beautiful you looked and about the baby you were carrying, and how our life would change so much with the birth of our first child. I hold on to the memory of that evening as one of the last times when our life was still so simple and uncomplicated. I love you!

When you came into my life, you made me complete. You taught me how to enjoy life. You make me feel special, like I am somebody. Until I met you, I never had anyone in my life who felt I was special, and who loved me as you do. We have come so far and grown so close together over the last twenty years. I cannot imagine my life without you. You are a devoted and loving wife and a wonderful loving mother.

My dear Adriana, I am not afraid of tomorrow, as long as you are at my side, hand in hand as we continue on our journey through life together. Our marriage is a merging of heart and soul that takes place over the course of a lifetime together. When I hold you in my arms and look into your eyes I feel so loved and have such a sense of belonging. Looking back over the years, it is awe-inspiring to reflect on how the two of us have come together in a way that made our life so complete and fulfilled. I cherish with all my heart the many wonderful memories I have of you from the first time we met, when we fell in love and all of the wonderful and heartwarming times we have shared together over the past twenty years of marriage. Like any couple, we have had our share of challenges, but through each challenge we have always found a greater closeness, a sense of harmony, and a deeper and more profound understanding of each other as our love stands the test of time. Each day I have with you is a blessing that I hold onto and cherish. You are the best part of my life, the source of my strength, and my greatest inspiration. Ours is a story that needs to be remembered as we pause once in a while on our journey, to embrace an aura from the past that breaks the boundaries of time and space to draw us back to special moments in our life. I dedicate this memoir to the many beautiful and cherished memories from a time when we first met and fell in love. I love you my dear Adriana with all of my heart and soul.

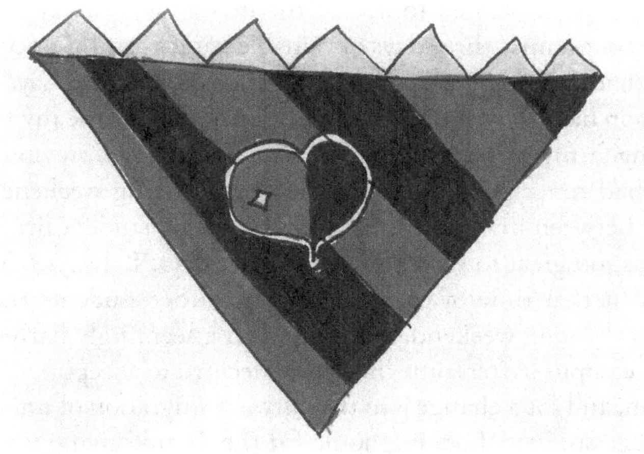

Chapter 1

The Journey Begins

Often brief moments can define one's destiny. Those are special moments that seem to hang suspended in time and space. At the time, they often seem insignificant; but in retrospect, they often stand out as some of the most important and life altering experiences. A cool autumn afternoon on October 8, 1988 was one such defining moment in my life. The colours of fall were starting to set in, as the trees were making ready for one final spectacular show before the onset of winter; the fall harvest was being collected, and horticulturists were savouring the last days of the season. It was the Thanksgiving weekend, and I was a third year political science and history student at the University of Waterloo. I was debating on accepting an invitation to celebrate the holiday at my uncle's house in Orangeville. I wanted to accept the invitation and yet did not want to compromise three days of valuable study time for upcoming lectures that I would have to sit through and research for essays that I would soon have to write. I almost decided to decline the invitation, but changed my mind at the last minute. Over the previous two years, I had never gone home for the Thanksgiving weekend. The distance between my home in the north and my student life in the south was too great to travel for a few short days. I always felt kind of lonely at that time of the year, as most other students traveled home for the long weekend, leaving me on a seemingly barren and deserted campus. After some thought, I decided to accept my uncle's invitation, and for a change join the outward migration of university and college students flocking home for the Thanksgiving weekend with family and friends. I did not know my extended family very well and had no friends in Orangeville; nevertheless, I was caught up in the overall excitement of the weekend. Floating along like a twig bobbing in the ebb and flow of a small stream, I could not have imagined the sudden change in direction the course of my life was about to make, as I unknowingly drifted into the outer fringes of a current. That current took hold of my life and opened my eyes to places that I had never seen. It was that day that I met the young woman whom I would come to love so much, marry, share my life, and raise my children with. Adriana was still a teenager when I first met her. She was nineteen years old, with only two days to go before her twentieth birthday. Looking back on that day, I now can hardly believe the transformation my life was about to make. It sometimes scares me when I think of what a fine line I walked in order for the events of that day to unfold and fall into place in a way that allowed me to meet the young woman who would become my life long companion and my most cherished friend.

For me, the day began with a free community pancake breakfast in the parking lot of the Town Square Mall in Waterloo. That morning I drove my 500 Honda Shadow motorbike to a friend's house, and we went to the Oktoberfest community breakfast together. I had known her for several years, and we had developed a very close friendship over the previous year and a half; however,

I had known for some time that we would be nothing more than friends.

After breakfast, I drove my motorbike to the St. Jerome College Residence to pick up my cousin Sanford. It was kind of exciting to think that I was now part of the outward migration of university and college students who were traveling home for the long weekend. Sanford was my Uncle Herman's son, and until that year I had not seen him since we were both young children at my grandparents' place in New Brunswick in the early 1970's. Now we were both students at the University of Waterloo and we met up again.

Chapter 2

The Encounter

It was a sunny cool autumn day as Sanford and I set out on our journey to Orangeville. Sanford sat on the back of my motorbike. As we got closer to Orangeville, Sanford started giving me more directions. He guided me through some of the back roads and shortcuts that led to his home. At that time, Orangeville was still very much a small town. The central business section of town was on Broadway Drive, the main street that ran through the center of town with a grocery store, a small sporting goods store run by a man almost as old as the town itself, a two-room movie theater, and a host of other small businesses that the town's people relied on for their day-to-day dealings. It was a simpler time when the town's main street was the place where people went shopping, took care of their daily business, and found their entertainment. Looking back, Orangeville was in the last days of innocence, as it sat on the verge of growing into something so much greater than anyone could have every imagined at the time. Sanford and I arrived at my Uncle Herman's house early in the afternoon, and there we met up with my other cousin, Caroline. She was a first year registered nursing student who never did graduate from the program. The three of us decided that we would go to the City Square Mall in Brampton for the afternoon. Unknown to me at the time, Caroline decided to invite her friend, Adriana, to join us for the afternoon. It was many years later that I learned Caroline's motive for that invitation: so that Adriana and I could meet. Of course neither Adriana nor I realized at the time that we were about to be introduced; nor could we have even begun to imagine how our lives were about to merge together.

Sanford, Caroline and I got into Uncle Herman's two-door white Dodge. Sanford was driving, I sat in the front seat on the passenger's side, with Caroline in the back behind Sanford. Once in the car, Caroline told me that we were going to pick up her friend, Adriana before going on to Brampton. On the trip to Adriana's house, I learned from Caroline that Adriana had immigrated to Canada from Romania. For some reason, I thought Caroline said Adriana was from Rhodesia, and to this day I am still convinced that Caroline said Rhodesia rather than Romania. At the time I remember it striking me as somewhat interesting to meet someone from Rhodesia. Throughout the drive, Sanford and I were discussing our dreams and visions for the future. Sanford was telling me of his plan to earn a law degree and a master's of business administration degree, and I told Sanford of my desire to purchase a Harley Davison and my hope to either go into law or the teaching profession, and without much thought, I also told him that I would someday like to become an elementary school principal. We were young and full of hope for the future. As we pulled into Adriana's driveway, I saw her mother, a short, stocky, somewhat graying woman in her early sixties. She was in her gardening clothes and wearing black rubber boots, and was working in the midst of an almost barren fall garden, turning over the soil as though she seemed to almost covet the last of her once- flourishing garden from the final fall harvest. I then saw Adriana for the first time, and it struck me that Caroline probably had meant to say Romania instead of Rhodesia, as I made the connection that Adriana was from an East European rather than an African nation. I was fascinated with her background. I was studying the East European communist political structures and culture at the time, and found it most intriguing to encounter a beautiful young woman who had lived behind the iron curtain under a communist regime.

When I saw Adriana she was beautiful and sexy and seemed so mysterious in a most attractive way. I can still see her walking towards me. She was stunning! As Adriana walked towards the car, I got out to let her in the backseat. That is when I first really saw her. As I stood there suspended in time, the seconds seemed to pass like minutes as I looked at this young woman walking toward me. I was breathless. Over twenty years later, I still remember what she was wearing. She wore a black leather mini skirt, black nylons and a black blouse with some black lace around the top that all seemed to work together to highlight her features. Her eyes had an almost oriental look, highlighted in black eyeliner with a tinge of purple trim and long black eyelashes, complemented by her high East European cheek bones. Everything from her long slender legs to her tall slim body was absolutely gorgeous. As Adriana came towards me, we smiled and said "Hi" to each other. She had been a landed immigrant in Canada for only three years at the time and still had a very strong accent that I found so alluring. I held the car door, as she moved her long slender body around me and settled into to the back seat. Our first encounter remains one of my most cherished memories, a moment suspended in time that holds a beauty all in itself. At that moment, when we first exchanged smiles, we had no idea of what we would come to share over the months and years ahead. It was not until years later that I learned from my son that Adriana thought I was handsome that day.

As we drove to Brampton, Sanford kept changing the radio stations. Each station was playing the same mid-eighties new wave songs. One specific tune I distinctively remember was, "Don't Worry, Be Happy". Adriana was sitting in the back seat just behind me moving her body along to the music while talking to Caroline.

She had an aura about her that was full of youthful energy and excitement, embodied in an element of mystery and innocence. I had trouble keeping my eyes off her and took every opportunity to look back at her without being too noticeable. Even from the passenger side of the car, I could often catch a glimpse of her eyes in the rearview mirror. I listened to every word that she said, and that was said to her, to learn as much as I could about this captivating young woman whom I had just met. I learned that she was a second year nursing student at Seneca College in Toronto, and that she was home visiting her family for the Thanksgiving weekend. Then finally came the question that I was waiting for: Sanford asked Adriana if she was still seeing her boyfriend. My heart began to sink until she spoke up and commented that she was not seeing anyone at the time, and that she and her boyfriend had broken up. I could not imagine how someone so gorgeous did not have a boyfriend, and more the point, how could anyone break up with such a stunning young lady? Nevertheless, this is what I wanted to hear. At the time, it seemed such a stretch of the imagination, to the point of almost being a dream, to think that we might span the gulf between us and combine our two lives together. It seemed almost too much to hope for. Years later Adriana told me that she actually did have a boyfriend and was sort of flirting with me a little when she informed Sanford that she and her boyfriend had broken up.

Sanford drove the four of us to the Square One Mall in Brampton. Adriana and I went our separate ways for the afternoon; she with my cousin Caroline, and I with Sanford. I remember thinking at the time that I would have sooner spent the afternoon following Adriana around the mall, than spending it with Sanford, as he shopped for some kind of preppy new watch. I remember making the point to Sanford that I did not rely on maintaining a timepiece to keep track of my days. After about two hours of window shopping, we all met at the front door of the mall. Adriana was carrying a small grey bag of items that she had purchased. She seemed to almost float as she moved along. She had a carefree manner that personified an air of youthfulness and purity that so captivatingly represented our way of thinking at the time. As we walked back to the car, Adriana spoke to me a second time. She asked me if I bought anything, and I responded by saying "No, I was just looking." It was only a short exchange of words, but it felt so good to talk with her. Back at the car we settled into our former seats, with Adriana sitting just behind me on the passenger's side. I would have given anything to sit in the backseat with her. On the return trip to my uncle's house, I remember admiring her accent, and taking every opportunity I could to catch a glimpse of her in the rearview mirror. Sometimes I only caught a short glimpse of her smile or a small segment of her face with the corner of my eye as she swayed to the music from the car radio while talking to Caroline.

We all drove back to my Uncle Herman's house. As the four of us walked from the car to the house, I made a point of walking beside Adriana. I was talking to her about my 500 Honda Shadow motorbike that was parked in Uncle Herman's backyard, and how Sanford and I rode the bike from Waterloo to Orangeville that morning. At first she seemed to think that I was talking about a bicycle and that was perhaps my fault, since I always referred to it as a bike. I clarified that it was a motorbike, and pointed to it in the backyard as we made our way to the side door of the house. I was hoping that she would want a ride, but I knew that I was expecting a little too much. At any rate, she did seem impressed with my bike.

Inside the house, Adriana, Aunt Dorothy, and Caroline sat in the kitchen talking, while Sanford and I talked in the dining room. I can remember keeping Adriana in the corner of my eye as she sat only a room's length away at the round oak kitchen table. I tried to think of some excuse that would allow me to move into the kitchen and sit at the table with her.

At that moment, Adriana pulled out of her grey plastic shopping bag a bottle of red wine that she had purchased that afternoon in celebration of her upcoming twentieth birthday. She invited Sanford and me to join her at the table for a toast. There were five of us in my uncle's house; but in my memory, I only really remember Adriana and me sitting at the table sipping the wine she had purchased. She was still nineteen years old at the time, since it was Saturday October 8, 1988, and her birthday was not until Monday the 10th.

As we all sat around the table toasting Adriana's upcoming twentieth birthday, I remember looking over at her as she tipped her glass back and closed her eyes. The almost oriental look of her half-oval-shaped closed eyes trimmed in black mascara and black eyeliner struck me as so beautiful and sexy. I have always admired the shape of her closed eyes.

Chapter 3

Evening Stroll

That evening Adriana and I went to the movie theater with my cousins at the old Uptown Theater on Broadway in Orangeville. The theater first opened in 1927 and remained open until 2002 when the modern multiplex theater with its metal siding, flashing lights and six inner theaters opened on the edge of town. Over the years the old Uptown Theater played old movies such as Gone with the Wind and many other silver screen classics that Adriana loved so much. It was a small town theater designed to mimic the larger New York theaters. The old architecture was filled with history, and no doubt was the site of many first dates and new loves throughout the decades. Over the years it never did display neon lighting, but simply had the word "Uptown" printed in large red letters over the front entrance. It was notorious for its late showing of movies, months after their box opening night dwindled from memory in the rest of the country. In its simplicity, it had an odd and almost romantic calling to the past, as it weaned out the last days of its existence in an ever-changing and modernizing world.

That evening we watched *Heartbreak Hotel*, a fictional story about Elvis Presley. I sat with Sanford, while Adriana and Caroline sat behind us. Adriana had changed from her black leather miniskirt and black lace trimmed top to a red dress that went down past her knees a little, with a black band around her waist. She looked so beautiful! The dress highlighted her features, everything from her shoulder length brunette hair, to her long gorgeous legs and her tall slender body. All I could think about during the movie was how much I wanted to be sitting with Adriana instead of Sanford.

Afterwards, the four of us were standing outside of the movie theater, and I made a point of standing beside Adriana and making small talk with her. I cannot remember what we were talking about; I just remember wanting to be near her as we walked side by side the short distance back to the car. I was so attracted to her! Her long slender body in that red dress looked so attractive under the night-lights of uptown main street. I will never forget our brief encounter during that brief walk side-by-side back to the car. It felt so good just to be walking beside her as we made small talk about a topic that has long since slipped into lost memories. That short stroll remains a treasured encounter within an enchanted and mystical moment for me in time and space.

Chapter 4

Ships Passing in the Night

Later that evening, I was in Uncle Herman's basement talking with Sanford and his friend while Adriana remained upstairs visiting. Both Sanford and his friend were first year students who were still excited about their new university life. It was mid term, and the workload had not hit them yet. From the basement I could hear Adriana talking and laughing upstairs and wished so much that I could find some excuse to move upstairs, so I could be in the same room with her. I wanted to spend more time with her before we each went our separate ways. I was afraid that I would not have an opportunity to see her again, and was already making plans, or creating reasons that would bring me back to Orangeville so that I would have an opportunity at a second chance encounter. As the last minutes of the day were slipping away, I could hear Adriana upstairs saying in her heavy Romanian accent "Goodbye," and wishing people a goodnight. I wanted to go upstairs to say goodbye to her, but was afraid it would seem too forward of me. To my pleasant surprise, before she went home for the night, she came down stairs to see Sanford and me. She looked around the door, announced that she was going home, and wished us a goodnight. She was still in her red dress. I remember admiring her jet-black hair, almond shaped sexy eyes, high cheekbones, long slender legs and her tall slim body. She looked so attractive, sexy, mysterious, and full of life in a manner that almost seemed to radiate a sense of youthful innocence. I remember thinking that her accent was so sexy and I was totally and completely captivated by her. After she left, Sanford's friend commented on how cute she looked, and I fully agreed. As she slipped out the door and into the darkness of the night, I was thinking of how much I would like to get to know her better, and wondered if I would ever see her again. It was almost a dream that I would even see her again, let alone manage to spend some time alone with her.

I went to sleep that night thinking about her, and I could not stop thinking about her over the next three months. I met Adriana in October, and it would take me until January to gain enough courage to ask her out on a date.

On Monday, October 10th Sanford and I retuned to Waterloo on my motorbike. I remember the day very well. It was a cold, wet, rainy morning. As we drove out of Orangeville on my 500 Shadow I seemed to feel a certain sense of loneliness that I did not understand. By the time we arrived in Guelph, Sanford was soaking wet and we were both very much chilled as the cool dampness of the day seemed to work its way deep into the aching crevasses of our bones. We stopped at a Subway restaurant at the junction of Highway 6 to warm up with a cup of coffee as I exchanged my somewhat waterproof jacket for Sanford's cold wet one. I arrived back at my apartment in Waterloo early in the afternoon on that damp, cold autumn day with an odd sense of emptiness that I had never really experienced before.

The memories of that Saturday afternoon, when I met Adriana for the first time, I hold dear to my heart. I am sometimes scared when I think of how near I came to not meeting her, and would have lost out on the richness that she brought to my life. I often think back to that day, and reflect on how the direction in my life changed so dramatically as a result of the course of events that were set to play on that autumn Saturday so many years ago.

Chapter 5

Trolling the Shoreline

When I was back in high school, my friend Nelson and I went on a weekend fishing trip alone on Kings Lake just a little south of Elliot Lake. Before returning to our tent for the night we were trolling with little luck. The water was calm; there was no wind, and we could feel the evening chill starting to settle in for the night. We were trolling the shoreline and were beginning to feel as if nothing much was going to come of our fishing trip other than a weekend in the bush. We actually thought of pulling in for the night, but decided to stay a little longer to make a few more runs in the deeper water farther from shore, as the darkness began to cover the landscape. Just as dusk slowly faded into a starlight sky, I felt like I had snagged the bottom, but then realized different as my rod bent and my line started unwinding at an alarming rate. After playing a back and forth game with the rod and real, I landed a ten-pound lake trout. By the time I landed the fish, we had stayed out on the lake much after sunset, and relied on a glow-stick marker that we had left in a tree on the shoreline near our tent to guide us ashore. Later that night we sat around the campfire, sharing a bottle of Captain Morgan and reflecting on our day's big catch.

Life can be a lot like our day on the lake. There can be times when you almost feel like giving up; and yet, if you are willing to make just a little more effort and take a few risks, things sometimes unexpectedly start to fall in place. The months following my first meeting with Adriana were something like that evening on the lake. I wanted the opportunity to meet her again on a chance encounter, but things just were not falling into place. Nor was I taking the necessary risks to make it happen. It was much like being back on the lake: I didn't land a big fish until I took some initiative and moved out into the deeper waters away from the safety of the shoreline.

The two months following my first acquaintance with Adriana were consumed with essay deadlines and final exams. In spite of these demands on my time, I made two attempts to meet Adriana again, before deciding that it was time to take some real initiative and risk. Otherwise, I rationalized, I may as well be content trolling the shallow shoreline with no real aspirations of any meaningful encounter beyond the dreams of better possibilities.

My first attempt to meet Adriana on a second chance encounter occurred a few weeks after Thanksgiving, when cousin Sanford and I traveled by train to Brampton enroute to Orangeville. We caught a Friday evening train at the downtown Kitchener terminal and sat across from two "older gentlemen" in their mid thirties. At least at the time I considered them to be older gentlemen. They were both highly astute insurance salesmen who immediately recognized Sanford and me as being university students. I think my University of Waterloo jacket might have been their first clue. They talked about their six-figure incomes and how life becomes much less exciting as one gets older – a prediction that never did transpire for Adriana and me.

No sooner had the train pulled into Brampton than Sanford and I made our way to a rather classy bar. He was going home for the weekend to go on a date with a young lady from a rather wealthy family, and I tagged along in the faint hope of a second chance contact with Adriana. Sanford talked to me a lot that evening about his high expectations for marrying into money, and discussed many of his heroes such as the Reichmann Brothers. A good part of our conversation that evening involved an explanation of how he planned to drop his family name and go simply with his first and second name, Sanford Kline, so his initials would be SK. It seemed that the family name, Underhill, was not quite classy enough for his grand expectations in life. He also talked a lot about how he already had the names for his children picked out. His son would be called Dakota, and the girl Indiana. Oddly enough, as things turned out, the only two things he failed to achieve from his list was to have a son and to drop his last name. We stayed at the bar a little too late, drinking and engaging in stormy university-level conversations that had little foundation in the real day-to-day trials and tribulations of mere mortals. While at the time we thought we were intelligent, we really had no idea what we were talking about, and did little more than to impress ourselves. Around 7 p.m. we realized that we missed our bus connection to Orangeville, and after a lengthy discussion of several options we agreed to split the cost of a stretched limo from Brampton to Orangeville.

We arrived in Orangeville around 9 p.m., and of course Sanford, whom I used to know as Sandy before he became too important for such a simple name, had to stop at the Beer Store, so that everyone could see him get out of a stretch limo and purchase a two-four. I sat in the back seat somewhat embarrassed by the spectacle he was making of himself, and equally grateful for the tinted glass that stood between him and me as he made his way to and from the Beer Store. I endured all this so that I might have an opportunity to meet Adriana again. Once at my uncle's house, I said very little but did listen a lot that weekend, and heard Adriana's name mentioned a few times. Caroline was talking about how Adriana liked to party a lot. I gathered from the kitchen table conversation that Adriana was not coming home that weekend, so I spent the two days in Orangeville with my uncle and his family. I went shopping in the morning with

Uncle Herman and my Aunt Dorothy at a small IGA store on main street near the movie theater, where Adriana and I had walked side by side only a few weeks earlier. Once back at the house, Caroline and a boarder named Ron joined us on a trip to the Square One Mall in Brampton, the same mall that I traveled to with Sanford, Caroline and Adriana that Saturday we first met. I walked around the mall but did not make any purchases. I had very little money in those days and became somewhat of an expert at window-shopping. My aunt purchased a rabbit fur coat that afternoon to wear to her daughter's graduation from nursing school only two short years away. Uncle Herman took us to dinner at a nice restaurant, and paid for everyone's meal. It was a really nice thing for him to do. He was a tall, slim man with graying hair. In his early sixties, he had a good work ethic and was employed at a truck loading dock in Brampton. He worked late hours loading trailers, and had not arrived home until the early hours of the morning.

The next day Herman drove Sanford and me back to the train station in Brampton. On the trip back Sanford explained that his date did not go that well. It seemed that the weekend was a disappointment for both Sanford and me. I appreciated the hospitality at my uncle's house; but nevertheless, was somewhat disappointed at my failed attempt to meet Adriana again.

A few weeks after my first failed attempt to meet Adriana again, I made one more trip to Orangeville to store my motorcycle at my Uncle Herman's house for the winter. My ulterior motive was, of course, to meet Adriana in a chance encounter, without having to make it obvious that I was looking to see her again. I was hoping that she would be visiting her family, and would take some time to meet with Caroline. I remember the ride as being very cold. It was in late November, and there was a danger of snow that evening. I left Waterloo late on a Friday night and had to stop mid way in Guelph at the Subway restaurant at the junction of Highway 6 to warm up. There was a real chill in the air that felt like winter was about to settle on the landscape. A young girl working at the sub shop told me that I might be in for some bad weather if I was going to travel too far north that night, as she saw a number of cars coming down Highway

6 covered in snow. I decided to continue on my trek in the hope of making it to Orangeville without running through any really bad weather. I could have stored the bike in Waterloo in my landlord's backyard, but took the invitation to store the bike at my uncle's house, with the faint hope of having an opportunity to meet Adriana again. It is hard to believe that when I returned to Orangeville the following Easter weekend to put the motorbike back on the road, Adriana and I had been dating for about four months and were only two months from our engagement. Caroline was home that November weekend when I arrived late in the evening almost frozen to my bike. I warmed up in the living room watching a movie on the life of Liberace with Caroline and her mother, as her mom lay on the couch drinking Pina Colodas. After the movie was over I made a point of inviting Caroline to Dairy Queen so I would have an opportunity to ask her about Adriana. We drove to Dairy Queen in her dad's car, and she told me that Adriana was not home that weekend, and that she very seldom returned home. Adriana's name did come up a few times that weekend in conversation between Caroline and her mother and I listened discreetly to every word to learn what I could about her. I really wanted to see her again and even to talk to her a little to get a sense of whether she might find me interesting enough to accept an offer for a date. I was really hoping for a chance encounter that just seemed beyond reach as I returned to Waterloo, again disappointed that I had not seen Adriana. Unfortunately, with my end-of-term exams approaching rapidly, I had to set aside any thoughts of meeting her again until after the Christmas holiday.

Chapter 6

Deeper Waters

Over the Christmas holiday's I returned to my parents' home in Elliot Lake. I caught a bus in Waterloo and changed buses in Toronto, as I made my way north to Sudbury where I caught a west-bound bus to the Elliot Lake turn off, and finally a small local school bus into town. The trek home was about an eight-hour ride, with several hours of layover time. I always loved stepping off the bus at the Sudbury terminal to feel the cold dry winter air of the north slamming into my face and grabbing hold of my lungs. It was such a refreshing change from the mild and damp winter days in Waterloo. The dampness of the southern winters seemed to settle into my bones and chill my body in contrast to the cold crisp winter air of the north that always felt so invigorating. When I stepped off the bus in Sudbury and felt the cold dry winter air on my face and deep down in my lungs, I knew that I was home.

In those days, returning home for the Christmas holidays or

March Break was like a big homecoming celebration. It was an opportunity to meet up with high school buddies, most of whom were also returning from college or university, or in Nelson's case trying for the third time in a row to complete grade thirteen. In those days I could walk through the mall on Christmas or New Years Eve or visit one of the local bars just about any night of the week and end up meeting most of my high school classmates. In no time, a small group would form, as we would all start sharing tales of our post-high school life. It was an exciting time; a coming of age. This was a special time in our life when we were completely free, with the boundaries of the adolescent years in the very recent past, and the confinement of life's real responsibilities fast approaching. It was an exciting time, when the only worries in life were final term grades and having enough pocket money for another drink at the bar.

The reunion with family and friends was exciting; however, at the same time that year it was a little different, as I fell into some deep soul searching. I realized that if I ever planned on seeing Adriana again I would need to step up to the plate and take some initiative; thus accepting the inherent risk that accompanies true initiative. Otherwise, I may as well be content with playing it safe with no real aspiration of ever seeing her again in any significant fashion. I decided that it was time to take a bold risk by leaving the shoreline and moving out into the deeper water. The first step was to cut ties to the past, and set my course of action. While in Elliot Lake, I said my final goodbye to two girls that were friends of mine, and told them both that I had met someone. One, a Swedish girl named Ann, whom I had known from high school and had gone out with a few times, called me one evening while I was home for the holiday. I had once turned down an invitation to have lunch in Toronto with her and the King of Sweden because I had an end-of-term paper due the following day. While home for Christmas that year, she invited me over to her apartment. I would often see her when I was home for the holidays; however, this time I informed her that I could not see her because I was dating someone. I wanted to cut ties with her and decided that this would be as good of a time as any. She put me on the spot by asking me whom I was dating, so I told her that I was dating Adriana. It seemed that my family may have overheard my conversation, so I simply told my parents that I met one of Caroline's friends and that she was from Romania. I did not say anything else, as there was nothing to say.

On another evening I was at a local bar having a few drinks with my friends John, James, and Val. Val was another girl I had known for a while, and in many ways she had helped to shape my destiny in a way that led me to Adriana. When I first met Val I was a grade twelve graduate in July of 1985, bound for a college business diploma program in Sudbury. I was somewhat intrigued by her in an odd sort of way. She told me all about a visit she made to the University of Waterloo and how impressed she was with the Arts Department. Her description of the Bachelor of Arts program at the University of Waterloo showed me an alternative to my previous plans, and I returned to high school the following day to register in the grade thirteen program with the intention of going to Waterloo. One year later we both found ourselves attending the University of Waterloo and became very good friends. Had I not met Valerie, I would not have attended the University of Waterloo; and consequently, I would not have met Adriana. It is odd how things sometimes unfold in ways that we cannot imagine at the time; and yet in retrospect, the road seems so clear and straight.

It was a cold crisp late December evening as John, James, Val and I left the bar for the long walk home. As we made our way home that evening, Val and I put some distance between the others and ourselves. We had been good friends for a while, and at times seemed to be almost dating – without really dating. It was kind of an odd relationship that was going nowhere in no real hurry. I told Val that I had liked her for a long time, but knew full well that there was really nothing between the two of us. After I explained to her that I had met someone special, we hugged each other that cold crisp December evening and assured each other that we would always be friends. Then we walked home in opposite directions. In the few brief encounters that we did have afterwards, I could almost sense that she missed the times that we had spent together. However, as time passed we continued to move in opposite directions until she disappeared into distant memories that are all but forgotten and faded with time.

I was taking a big chance, as I had no real idea if Adriana would really want to see me again, and was very much hoping that she still was not dating anyone. At any rate, I knew that I was in limbo, and I had to move forward. If things were not to work out, I at least had freed myself to move on with my life. I also knew that if I did not at least take a chance to try to make something happen, I would be left wondering what if? What if I did ask her out and what if she did like me? What if things really did work out for the two of us? I needed to move out from the safety of my familiar surroundings and make things happen.

Chapter 7

Return to Waterloo

On my return to Waterloo after Christmas, I finally got the courage to call Caroline and ask for Adriana's phone number. My intentions were made clear, and it was going to be all or nothing. I remember Caroline laughing a lot as we talked. She told me that Adriana had been seeing someone, but had recently broken up with him. I knew that she was not seeing anyone when we met over the Thanksgiving holiday and found it a little odd that she had started dating someone and broke up so soon: and yet was grateful that at least she was not dating anyone at the present time.

After saying good-bye to Caroline, I tried to wait until my roommate was out of earshot before calling Adriana. I sat in our basement apartment, as he seemed to be lingering around for an eternity, until finally after about five minutes of waiting I told him I was calling a girl, and to please not laugh if I got shot down. I thought about what I was going to say, took a deep breath and called her. Adriana's voice sounded so sweet on the phone. I loved her accent and could not believe that I was actually talking to her. Even more, I could not believe that she accepted my invitation for a date. I introduced myself by telling her that I was Caroline's cousin, and reminded her that I met her over the Thanksgiving weekend. What a sigh of relief when she said she remembered me! I asked her if she would like to go out that coming weekend, and she accepted. We talked a little about where we would meet, and both agreed that she would come to Waterloo the following Saturday and I would meet her at the Kitchener Greyhound bus station around 4 p.m. She had a friend in Kitchener with whom she could stay with for the weekend. I was so excited after our conversation on the phone. I could not believe that I was going on a date with such a beautiful young woman. The gorgeous girl that sat behind me in the Orangeville Uptown Theater in the fall would now be actually sitting beside me in the Kitchener theatre – as my date. As I hung up the phone and expressed my excitement, my roommate, John McDonald noted that long distance relationships never seem to work, and reminded me that she lives in Toronto, and I live a hundred kilometers away in Waterloo. However, I was on a natural high that even his perpetual pessimistic pose could not deter.

As I began to plan the date, I started thinking of some of the places that I knew in Kitchener and decided to start the evening with dinner at a Chinese restaurant named Lai Lai's that John McDonald, Jay Churchill and I went to a year earlier. Then we would go to a movie and end the evening at Lou Lou's, a bar on the outskirts of town. As the week went by I thought about our upcoming date, and decided that perhaps it was time for a few changes in my own life. Since grade three I wore my hair long, and decided that that was something I wanted to change. I really wanted to impress Adriana, and decided to cut my hair short. I thought that she, having come only a few short years ago from a communist nation, would like a cleaner cut look. As the week went by, I remember having lunch with a friend from school, John Hommes. We talked a little about my upcoming date, not realizing at the time that in less than a year Adriana and I would be inviting him to our wedding.

Chapter 8

The Well

I remember, years later, sitting in a small rural Catholic parish with Adriana and our two children on a Sunday morning. The priest talked about how God reveals elements of eternal bliss in our daily lives, through often very brief glimpses of breathtaking beauty that seem to transcend time and space to enlighten our mortal realm. This revelation could come in the form of a stunning pinkish sunset over a calm clear lake, walls of aurora borealis dancing in the midnight sky, reflections of light on the dew of an early spring morning or even in an exchange of kindness between two strangers. These are almost magical experiences that momentarily elevate us out of our everyday life, briefly enlightening our very perception of our surroundings. These memories are the places we drift to in our mind when we need to return to our foundations to be refreshed for the challenges of life, much like the passion of new love that endures the test of time and evolves into something greater, as two people come together and truly merge as one. Sometimes those early days of a new relationship, the foundation of what is to come, fade into a distant memory that becomes blurred and forgotten over time with the hustle and rush of daily life and kitchen table talk. Once in a while we need to stop and look back to where we came from and treasure those lost days of our youth, when we were young and newly in love, a time when we were elevated beyond the monotony of our daily surroundings that at can so often seem to clog our very existence. Those early days, when two people first come together and get to know each other, are hidden treasures locked in our memories. They are the wells we return to for hope and refreshment as we recall cherished moments from the past, those foundations on which the lives of two people began to merge together. It is a time of innocence and awkwardness, a time when things we take for granted later in a relationship such as a kiss or holding hands were not taken for granted. A time of excitement and passion as two people come together and lay the foundations for sharing a life together. Those early days of a new love when a young couple first meet, their first date, the first time they hold hands, their first kiss and first dance – these are treasured memories that we draw on when the storms of life roll in and seem to drown us in the monotony and challenges of our daily existence.

I first called Adriana on a Monday evening, and the week seemed to pass by so slowly, until finally it was Saturday, January 28, 1989. That afternoon I found myself sitting in a big armchair in my basement apartment watching a World War II movie based on an American air assault on Japan in the days that followed Pearl Harbor. It was an old black and white movie based on a true story. Following the Japanese attack on Pearl Harbor the Americans made a bold move by launching bombers in the mid Pacific from an aircraft carrier. They were to attack Japan, and then crash land in China, since they had no friendly airstrips in range. It was one of the bolder and more daring moves by the Americans during the Second World War. I was sort of half watching the movie and half watching the time go by until finally at about 2 p.m. I turned the television off I never did see the end of that movie. I caught a city bus to the Kitchener Gray Coach terminal and waited for Adriana to arrive from Toronto on the 4 p.m. bus. I was leaning with my back to the wall when she stepped off the bus. We saw each other and sort of half waved as we awkwardly moved towards each other and talked a little. She looked stunning in her acid-wash jean jacket, black corduroy pants and white blouse. We took a taxi to her friend's apartment, so that she could drop off her suitcase. From there, her friend's brother drove us to the Chinese restaurant somewhere down Victoria Street.

At the restaurant we were taken to a booth tucked away in the corner somewhat isolated from the rest of the restaurant, and ordered our meal. We didn't eat much, as there was an air of awkward nervousness that often arises when we walk in uncharted territory, unsure of what we will find around the next bend, wanting to let down our armor, but afraid of exposing our vulnerability. I only remember small pieces of the conversation. I talked a bit about some of the places I lived as a child. I can really only remember the two of us looking at each other in the dim candlelight of the restaurant, and feeling so amazed that the girl I met in Orangeville last fall was here on a date with me, and wondering whether or not she liked me as much as I liked her. Questions ran through my mind. Can I hold her hand? Can I kiss her? Will we make any kind of meaningful connection? These are the things that we take for granted later in life and yet are aspects of such anticipation and uncertainty on a first date.

After dinner we walked down Victoria Street and took a right on King Street, past the downtown mall and on to the movie theater. It was now dark. The two of us walked together under the streetlights as two solitudes, not more than a few inches apart, winding our way under the softly lit streetlight on that memorable, mid-winter evening. There was a real sense of wanting to be closer, balanced by a hesitation founded in uncertainty and awkwardness as we cautiously felt our way down this new and unmapped path. It was a very mild January evening, allowing us to walk dressed in late fall clothing. As we talked, I learned that Adriana's father had passed away a few years previous from cancer, before she immigrated to Canada at age sixteen. She spoke very little English when she first arrived, and even at the time of our first date she still had to stop and think a little about how she would word things in English. Her accent and the way she had to sometimes stop and think before she spoke was so appealing. She told me that her father worked as a mechanic in a Romanian chemical factory and had visited Canada a few months before his death. She also told me that she planned on purchasing a Porche when she completed her nurse's training. Even though I learned a lot about her as we walked under the faint streetlights that winter evening, she was still wrapped in a cloak of mystery. The more I learned of her, the more I wanted to know her, but in the end, it took many years to really get to know and understand her.

As we walked together we talked until we finally arrived at the movie theater on King Street in downtown Kitchener. We looked over the posters advertising the current showings and decided which movie we would watch. I don't remember much about the selection, other than the movie, Naked Gun with Leslie Neilson. After a short discussion and one Freudian slip on Adriana's part, we decided that Naked Gun would be the movie for us. When I asked her which movie she would like to see, she responded by informing me that she would like to see Naked Men! Realizing her error, she looked a little embarrassed as she rolled her eyes to the right and said in her heavy Romanian accent, "Oh my God, I mean Naked Gun!"

I will never forget the ninety minutes we spent in that movie theater together. It was the time when we first held hands. We were sitting in the darkness of the theater when she reached over and took hold of my hand. She was the first girl that I ever took to the movies. As we sat in the shadows of the theater, she put her hand into my hand and our flesh touched. This is one of my most cherished memories. I think I must have held her hand for the rest of the evening. I do not remember much of the movie, other than just sitting with her in the darkness of the room. In my memory it almost seems like we were alone.

After the movie, we walked down the street talking, hand in hand, and I held her hand as much as I could for the rest of the evening. After about a half hour we found a phone booth and called for a taxi to take us to Lou Lou's. As we stood by the roadside still holding hands, a somewhat intoxicated man walked past us, and yelled something about the USSR. We sort of looked at each other as he passed, and then our taxi arrived.

Lou Lou's boasted having the longest bar in the world. It was about one mile in length and has long since closed. When we arrived we walked around the bar a little lost before I purchased two bottles of Canadian and moved over to a table for two where we sat down and only drank about a third of our beer. We could not talk much because the music was so loud, but I watched as Adriana sat across from me smiling and swaying her head and whole upper body to the beat of the music. After a few minutes she took me by the hand and said, "Let's dance," as she led me hand-in-hand to the dance floor. As our bodies slowly came together I held her close to me, with both my arms around her tall slender body and my hands rested on her lower back, just above her jeans while I rested my right cheek on the side of her head. She had both of her arms around my upper body as we pulled in close and tight to each other, slowly swayed back and forth to the music, without really moving anywhere. We danced a lot that evening, and it felt so good holding her body in close to mine. As we held each other on the dance floor we kissed for the first time. I will never forget that kiss. As we were dancing Adriana put her lips to mine. There must have been a thousand people around us, and yet when our lips touched there was no one else – just us. No matter the type of music, we just held each other close and kissed for the rest of the evening. That is a memory that I will cherish for the rest of my life. With our bodies in tight to each other and slowly swaying to the music, Adriana pulled back from me for an instant, and looking at me with her big beautiful brown eyes, asked, "Wouldn't you sooner be here with a pretty girl?" While still swaying back and forth to the music, I gently placed my hands on either side of her face and whispered in her ear, "I am here with a pretty girl," and continued dancing as she moved in close to me again. All evening I just kept looking at her and thinking to myself, "Adriana is so beautiful, and she is my date." I could not believe that this gorgeous girl with her long beautiful slender body and sexy East European accent that I had met and dreamed about for the past four months was with me, holding my hand, dancing with me, and kissing me. All that evening I was overwhelmed and almost at times in disbelief that she was actually on a real date with me and so attracted to me. I had hoped to go on a date with her for so long and at times had been afraid that I might never see her again after we first met on that cool crisp autumn day only four months previous. We stayed at Lou Lou's a few hours, until closing time, and caught a taxi back to her friend's apartment building.

Back at the apartment we sat in a somewhat secluded area, near the main entrance and kissed for about ten minutes. I then walked her to the elevator where we kissed again and said goodnight. I watched her as the door closed, and wondered if I would ever see her again. As I tried to find my way out of the building, I got a little turned around, and arrived back at the elevator where I had left Adriana only a few moments previous. The door opened, and when I looked up, there was Adriana standing in the elevator. We kissed each other goodnight again before we each found our way home for the night. As I walked away I looked back once in vain, hoping the door would open again, and see Adriana standing there one more time.

As I walked home I thought about our date. I thought about everything from meeting her at the bus station, to our meal at the Chinese restaurant, the movie, dancing, holding hands and kissing. I could not believe that I was on a date with such as beautiful girl. It seemed so long ago that I had met her and we walked side by side down main-street in Orangeville on that cool autumn evening. She was still a mystery to me, as I knew so little of her; who she was, where she came from and what she hoped for in her future; and yet, I was closer to her that night than I had ever been with anyone, and I did not want the evening to end. I was so afraid that perhaps she would not want to see me again. I fell in love with her that night. All I knew was that I wanted to be with her as much as possible for the rest of my life.

Over twenty years later, I still feel the same, and I am more in love with her now than ever. I cherish the memories of our first date. That was the night I held her hand, and our lips first touched. She made me feel so special! I was and still am so in love with her!

Chapter 9

The Day After

Then came the next magical day. I was so happy when she called me and wanted to spend the day with me. She decided to stay in Kitchener for another day and catch the Monday morning bus back to Toronto. We agreed to meet at the Town Square Mall. I walked down to the mall in a misty winter rain and waited for her by the mall entrance. She arrived in a taxi five minutes later. As she stepped out of the taxi we made our way towards each other, and once again experienced a somewhat awkward moment, as we talked a little before embracing each other and kissing in the empty parking lot. It was a cold wet Sunday morning in late January and we were all alone kissing in the rain. We laughed a little, took each other by the hand, and ran over to the protection of the mall as we held each other close in the rain, partially protected from the elements by the overhang on the side of the building where we embraced again in a long kiss. As we kissed we moved in as close as we could to the side of the building to take shelter. I had hoped that we would kiss again, but until we did I was afraid that perhaps she was having second thoughts about me. It felt so good to be so close with her, and to know that she still wanted to be with me.

We decided to go back to my place and watch some movies. I had a small two-bedroom basement apartment that I shared with John McDonald. On the taxi ride back to my apartment, we held hands in the backseat. I remember moving my thumb around to feel her hand. I learned years later that it had really annoyed her, but it felt so good to have her hand in mine. Once back at my apartment, Adriana noticed that I had a stack of dirty dishes in my sink like she had never seen before. Without saying much, she walked into the kitchen and washed each dish. I knew then that I found someone special!

Sitting with her in my living room that evening, I cannot remember which movies we watched; I think one was called The Black Widow. I only remember being so happy that she was with me. I was even happier when John McDonald decided not to watch the second movie, and left us alone. But we didn't watch much of the second movie, as we lay on the couch and kissed some more. It felt wonderful being so close to her; and more to the point, I could not believe that such a beautiful girl wanted to be with me. It was a time of innocence when holding each other embraced in a kiss was exciting and new, as our bodies pushed together wanting more, but not going too far.

I didn't want the weekend to end. I wanted it to last the rest of my life. I never knew what it felt like to be truly happy and to feel like I truly belonged with someone until that weekend. But alas, it did end, and too soon as she took a taxi back to her friend's apartment later that evening. The next day I went to a flower shop in the Westmount Plaza on the way to school, and sent her half a dozen red roses.

Those first two dates were special - embraced in awkward simplicity they were beautiful in their own right and yet they also provided a glimpse into something that was to evolve beyond the comprehension of two youth lost in the purity of a new and fragile beginning.

Chapter 10

Shutting Doors and Opening Windows

Sometimes unanswered prayers are our greatest gifts. For a moment our world can seem to unwind and fall apart, leaving us to wonder how such tragedy could befall us. Yet, in retrospect, it is sometimes those very tragedies that shape our destiny in ways that only become evident with the passage of time. As we reflect on our life, we are often faced with the truth that many of our greatest blessings and gifts actually formed in the dust and aftermath of tragedy and suffering.

Adriana and I agreed that we would spend the next weekend together in Kitchener, since she had an open invitation to stay with her friend. However, on Monday evening Adriana called me in tears, telling me that she had failed her nursing exam and would have to leave the program. I remember telling her not to worry about it, as she could always do it over again. She offered to back out of our date. Since she failed her program she thought that I would not want to see her anymore. I told her at that point that I loved her, and still wanted to see her. There followed an awkward silence.

She came to see me the following Friday in the mist of a captivating, cold, crisp snowy weekend that seemed almost magical. I met her at the bus stop as I had done the week before, only this time when she stepped down from the bus I greeted her by holding both her hands and kissing her, followed by a long embrace. From the bus stop we walked hand in hand down King Street. She was wearing a pink winter jacket, acid-wash jeans, and white leather boots. We walked under the hazily lit streetlights, often stopping momentarily to embrace in a long passionate kiss. No matter where we where, it was as if we were all alone with no concern or consideration for onlookers. We went to the movies, followed by a late evening meal, before I escorted her to her friend's home at the conclusion of our date. I do not remember much else of that weekend, other than her slippery boots. There were several times when she almost fell and I had to catch her. And catching her was an enjoyable part of the evening, as she would slip and end up in my arms. With my winter break fast approaching we agreed that weekend that Adriana would accompany me home to Elliot Lake for my winter leave. We decided to meet in Toronto, and catch the train north the following Saturday.

The next week Adriana and I talked on the phone a few times before we met Saturday morning in Toronto, and I sent her another half dozen roses for Valentine's Day. Adriana could probably count on her fingers how many times I brought her flowers over the course of our dating and marriage to follow. In general I tend to regard flowers as too perishable a gift and truly feel that a real gift should be something that lasts – like jewelry that a woman could cash in at a hockshop if she so desires. Nevertheless, sending Adriana a half dozen roses for our first Valentine's Day together seemed like the right thing to do at the time, and as the years passed I came to better appreciate the value that women place on receiving flowers from a man. While the flowers were a nice touch that came from my heart, I did forget to buy her a Valentine's Day card. In a panic I dropped into a card store in Waterloo on February 15, 1989 to purchase a

Valentine card, only to realize that all the cards had been stored away that morning. However, the young women working at the store were very kind, and let me look through boxes of cards in the back room, as they no doubt thought to themselves, "He's in trouble!"

The upcoming week in Elliot Lake was a much-anticipated occasion. It was the time when I first introduced Adriana to my family, and a time that we started to grow very close together, as we moved from just dating to developing a commitment towards each other. This was a special time in our life that would not have happened if Adriana had remained in her nursing program that year. From that week, there grew a beautiful life together, eventually with two wonderful children and a lifetime of sharing, love, and companionship.

Chapter 11

Meet the Parents

With my winter break finally before me, I caught a city transit from the University of Waterloo to downtown Kitchener, where I transferred to a Toronto-bound Grey Coach. As the bus made its way to Toronto, I was filled with anticipation of the day and the week to come. I was so captivated by Adriana; and yet she was still such a mystery to me that I looked forward to spending my winter break with her and getting to know her better. As the Grey Coach made its way off Highway 401 and into the core of the city, my excitement grew, knowing that in a few short minutes I would be holding Adriana in my arms again. Toronto was still very foreign to me, but I did recognize the bus terminal area as I had made many transfers in that building on route between Sudbury and Kitchener over the previous two years. Finally, as the bus approached the corner of Elizabeth and Dundas, somewhat dwarfed by the surrounding architecture, the low- profile two storey grey concrete bus terminal with its black trimmed upper and lower windows and its high arched front entrance came into sight.

It was a cool and damp February morning in Toronto, as the bus made its way onto the loading platform. I could see Adriana waiting for me off to the side of the terminal. She looked so gorgeous with her long slender form covered by her black wool overcoat and a white knitted winter hat, pulled tight over her jet-black hair. She carried a small black backpack over her left shoulder and had a rather large green leather suitcase at her side, as she patiently waited for my arrival from Waterloo. As I stepped down from the bus, with a certain level of awkwardness and excitement, we made our way towards each other. Our bodies and lips slowly merged together in a long and silent embrace. For that short time, the hustle and movement of the city around us seemed to vanish as we became lost in our own world. Pulling back a little, I put my hands on either side of her rosy high-boned cheeks and told her how happy I was to see her again. Even today, I can still see her there; she looked absolutely gorgeous; and thinking back to that morning twenty-one years ago, I remember I had a hard time even believing that she was with me. As we took hold of our luggage I can remember her commenting that she brought such a large suitcase for the week, and all I had was a small backpack.

With only an hour before the departure of the north-bound Via Rail Train, we headed for the train station. I held tight onto Adriana's hand while she led me down Dundas to the Young Street subway line, where we walked down a long set of stairs leading from the sidewalk to the underground platform. I had only been on a subway a few times in the past. As a small town boy from the north I found riding the subway such an intimidating experience. The trains seemed to come into the station with such speed and moved out so rapidly that I worried that we might become separated if I did not move fast enough at the boarding and offloading points. Standing a good distance back from the edge of the platform, I held Adriana's hand and waited for the train to arrive. In no time it flew in like a bullet; we boarded and barely took our seat before it shot off again like a silver streak into the darkness of the black hole at the end of the platform. The underground made only two short stops – one at the Queen Street platform and other at King Street, before we pulled into Union Station in what seemed like only a five-minute transit. As the train came to a stop, Adriana and I stood up and made our way, hand in hand, to the door. I remember being a little worried about not getting off the train in time, and finding myself all alone whipping along the seemly endless tunnels of the Toronto underground, with no idea of how to find my way back again. Adriana could tell that I was uncomfortable making my way around Toronto, and stayed close to me.

At the base of the Young Street line, Union Station was an impressive three-storey concrete building lined with huge concrete pillars. As we walked from the subway platform into the station, I was struck by the impressive state of its architecture. Once inside the building we found ourselves walking across a huge rectangular room with a three-storey-high arched ceiling and a high clear glass arched window at the far end of the building. It must have been at least two storeys high. Walking hand in hand with Adriana through this massive open concept building, I felt like I had just walked into a cathedral. We moved around Union Station a little lost before we found our way to the Via Rail gate, only to learn that the train was delayed. Since Adriana had such a large suitcase, we decided to just wait there at the gate holding hands and catching up. At first we were the only passengers in line, but as time passed, the queue grew longer and longer behind us. As we stood there talking I learned that her rather large green leather suitcase had a bit of history. It was the suitcase that her father used on a visit to Canada several years ago, a few months before his death, and the same suitcase that Adriana used when she immigrated to Canada. Since then, Adriana had never ventured far from the Toronto region, and now, after dating me for less than a month, she was accompanying me to my parents' home in the far north. If she was a little on edge about meeting my family, she hid it well. The time passed quickly for us that afternoon. Whenever we were together it seemed like time just slipped away. By mid-afternoon we found ourselves standing at the front of a long line of passengers waiting to board the train, and that was exactly where I wanted to be. We had economy class tickets with no assigned seating. I wanted to make sure we were some of the first passengers to board the train, so that we could sit together for the trip north. I didn't want to even think of the possibility of finding myself being one of the last passengers to walk on the train, and being assigned seats in different parts of the train. Finally, we were led down a lengthy corridor and into a long dark bay. The ceiling was lined with two rows of skylights that ran the length of the bay, with several tracks leading out of the far end of the dark hallway into the light of day. Following a Via Rail employee, we made our way down one of the concrete platforms that line the track, beside a blue train trimmed with a yellow line that ran down its mid section. As we boarded the train, we stored Adriana's large suitcase on a luggage rack at the back of the car and placed our small backpacks in the overhead luggage compartment.

We found a seat alone near the back of the car. Adriana sat beside the window and I took the one on the aisle. I put my arm around her shoulder, and she nestled into me as our lips met. The train took a while before it finally pulled out of Union Station, and we passed the time in each others' arms. Once underway, the train emerged from the darkness of the bay into daylight and made its way through the city and into the surrounding snow-covered fields of Southern Ontario's farm belt. It was an exciting time for the two of us. After dating for only a few weeks, we were going on a one-week vacation together, meeting my family. For Adriana, this was her first time traveling outside of the Southern Ontario region since she arrived in Canada as a landed immigrant only a few short years ago. As the train chugged its way across the fields, Adriana and I exchanged Valentine cards. She also presented me with a red loose-stitch sweater with a large leather patch on the chest that read "Frontier." I kept that sweater for years afterwards. I felt bad, because I did not have a gift for her.

After a short while we moved to the back of the train where we settled ourselves into the dome car, snuggling close to each other in our seats. Nestled into each other, watching the passing countryside through the mid-winter frost trimmed windows, I clearly remember, twenty years later, enjoying our conversation that day and the sincere joy of Adriana's company. We stayed in the dome car until sometime after sunset when the car started to actually chill down, causing us to move back to our assigned seating in the economy class. While making our way from the coolness and openness of the dome car to the warmth and seclusion of our isolated economy seat only two cars away we were caught by the night conductor when we stopped for a kiss in the narrow corridor just past the bar car. Thinking we were alone, our young thin bodies molding into each other, our lips merging, we were lost in each others' arms, when the conductor found himself blocked by our passionate embrace as he attempted to make his way down the narrow corridor. Encouraging us to move along, in a somewhat humorous yet stern tone of voice, he said, "There's no room for young love in a narrow corridor!" With a rather large conductor on our heals, I took Adriana by the hand, and we moved along to the semi-seclusion of our seat at the back of the car, where we were a little more free to talk and kiss without holding up traffic.

As the train chugged along piercing the darkness of the cold fridged night, Adriana and I shared in the warmth of each others' company our dreams and hopes for the future. After dating for only a few weeks, this was the first time that we really talked to each other and shared our aspirations. Adriana told me that she had wanted to be a nurse since she was a young girl and looked forward to completing her nursing program. I remember telling her that I was hoping to work in municipal government administration. Having said that, my vision for the future was for the most part undecided, and my response in particular to career prospect questions changed depending on the time of day, month or year anyone talked to me regarding my future career plans. In fact, I only ended up in teaching because it was raining one morning in Toronto. I was cutting grass for Walter's Landscape in Toronto the first year Adriana and I were married. When my shift was cancelled one morning due to rain, I decided to make my way to the University of Toronto and apply to the Bachelor of Education program, a decision that resulted in me teaching for several years before finding myself as an elementary school principal - first in Muskrat Dam, Ontario and then in Behchoko, Northwest Territories. In contrast to Adriana, I never really had a plan; I just sort of fell into life. I always admired Adriana for being so focused on what she wanted and where she wanted to go in life, in contrast to me, who followed a more organic approach, altering decisions and choices as events unfolded. Adriana knew what she wanted to do with her life from the time she was a little girl, and she stayed the course.

As the train slowly made its way north, Adriana asked me about my plans for the future, and in particular if I wanted a house and children when I am married. I remember thinking that those things seemed so far in the future, especially for a poor university student with little money; nevertheless, I did tell her that someday I did want to own a home and have children. The train slowly wound its way through the Canadian Shield and into Sudbury in the darkness of the night, ending our six-hour ride. We enjoyed every minute of the trip, nestled into each other in the solitude of our seat.

When we stepped off the train in Sudbury we were hit with the cold northern winter winds of February. It always felt so refreshing to return to the north in the winter. The southern winters were always slushy, mild and humid. The north was cold, dry and crisp. Standing on the Sudbury Via Rail platform in mid February with that coldness on my face and the cold crisp northern air penetrating deep down in my lungs, I knew I was home. I helped Adriana down from the train, and found my brother and his girlfriend's brother waiting for us. In those days the train station was still in downtown Sudbury. The old traditional train station was similar to so many other stations that marked the center of many towns across this country. This particular station was built in 1907 by the Canadian Pacific Company only twenty-five years after the railroad first wound its way through the Sudbury area, and actually opened Sudbury as the nickel capital of the world. It was a long brick building trimmed in stone with a hip-roof profile and a rather large portico extending off the edge of the building. Over the years the station slowly descended from a place of business, transportation and communication to becoming simply a warm place in the middle of winter for some of the local street people to spend an evening. The station had declined over the years into a somewhat seedy establishment, with its grand structure towering over its shabby dilapidated walls and its faded blue plastic seats besieged by a multitude of seemingly lost and wondering souls. Yet even in those last few years of service, the old station still captivated an aura of grandeur as it held on with an ever-slipping grip to spirits of the past in an ever-changing and modernizing world, unlike its successor - a small corrugated metal structure on the outskirts of town at the end of a gravel laneway that became known as simply, "The Sudbury Junction." We didn't realize it at the time, but the world around us was changing and we were changing with it.

As we walked across the platform, I stopped to introduce Adriana to my brother John, and Glen, his friend. Glen was a tall, slim dark haired man with a thin beard that lined his jawbone and upper lip. Several years later, when Adriana and I lived in North Bay, we actually became quite good friends with him. At that time in our lives we had a dingy upper apartment in a somewhat decaying old home on Jane Street. That was during my Bachelor of Education studies, and Glen lived a block away in a basement apartment while completing his diploma in business administration. We used to meet once in a while for coffee in a funky little coffee shop that was more like a general store with a few tables.

John was only eighteen years old. In those days my brother had an almost blond Afro- like hair-do and wore a black leather jacket. He was a little shorter than I am, standing just shy of six feet tall; he was very slim and always had a cigarette hanging out of his mouth. He had dropped out of high school, or rather was asked to leave by Mr. Riddle, the vice principal. John had settled into the pizza delivery service with the aid of his little blue Ford Escort. In many ways John seemed lost and it took many years for him to find himself. He was much more rambunctious than I ever was and seemed to always be on the fringe of somewhat seedy associations. I loved him, and worried a lot about what would ever become of his life. He was a good- natured person who was quick to help his friends and family. He knew how to wheel and deal, and he did it well; someone once said that, "John could sell a freezer to an Eskimo," and it was true. He had a way of making things sound good, even when you knew in your heart that it wasn't. As the years passed he did fine for himself, first as a long-haul truck driver and then as an electrician, but most importantly as a good father to two beautiful children, Brayden and Annabel.

For the journey home to Elliot Lake, Adriana and I settled into the backseat of John's little blue Escort. It was a tight fit, but neither of us seemed to mind, as I put my arm around her and she snuggled into me for the two-hour ride home. Adriana noted that the narrow windy road to Elliot Lake reminded her of her home in Romania. Since her arrival in Canada, she had never ventured this far from Toronto and was not aware that Canada also had winding hillsides like her home country.

When we arrived in Elliot Lake, John drove us to my parents' home, where I introduced Adriana to the rest of my family. I had a large family in which I was the eldest of two boys and three girls. My parents were pleasant people. My father grew up on a farm near Matheson, a small town in Northern Ontario, and my mother was from Barnettville, a tiny village in New Brunswick. My father had spent many of his early years as a mine accountant and sometimes as an underground miner; however, he gradually moved over to fulltime accounting as he settled down with a family. Since he never did complete his professional papers, his pay was always quite low for the type of work he was doing. My mother, on the other hand, was a registered nurse but remained at home for many years raising her five children before returning to the nursing profession after my dad was forced from the workplace in the wake of a heart attack and several mini strokes.

I had a very good relationship with all of my family, and this was a very special moment for me. It was not often that I brought someone home, so they knew that this must be someone special to me. I remember my family asking Adriana about her home country, her family and commenting on her being a friend of Caroline Underhill. Shortly after arriving, Adriana called her sister to let her know that she had arrived safely, as her sister was concerned about Adriana making the journey north, since Adriana's family did not know my family. As she talked on the phone, my family seemed impressed with the sound of Adriana speaking her language. My mother actually asked me, "Is that her language?"

After this my Dad took out a world atlas, and Adriana showed everyone where she was from. She pointed to a small town called Tarnaveni somewhere in central Romania, a place that Adriana and I would visit on two occasions in the not-too-distant future. Built partly on the flood plains of the Tarnava Mica River located about 45 kilometers from Targu-Mures, it is an ancient community in central Mures. Its origins date back almost to the beginning of the previous millennium. Over the years it had changed names several times - known in 1259 as Terra Dycheu and then later referred to as Weinland in recognition of its rolling hillsides covered with a multitude of vineyards. Tarnaveni was the site of a battle during which two hundred Romanian soldiers defended the community from the retreating soldiers of the Third Reich, following Romania's shift in allegiance from the Axis powers to the Allies during the dwindling days of Second World War. The gravesite of the soldiers who perished in that battle can still be visited in Tarnaveni. Through the center of town ran the Blaj-Praid railroad, that as a child Adriana crossed on her way to and from school. She used to tell me of how she would cross the tracks by walking between the rail cars, something that I considered a little dangerous. Following the Second World War the town underwent an industrial boom with the discovery of methane gas deposits and the construction of a glass and chemical factory that her father worked at as a mechanic. As the community continued to grow in the post-war years, numerous young people moved to the community from the surrounding rural villages looking for employment and a life in an urban environment. For some people the move to an urban centre was their own choice, but for others the communist regime's focus on developing Romania's urban industrial sector forced this change upon them. It was this urban migration in the mid 1960's that brought Adriana's parents to Tarnaveni where they met, were married, and raised their family. Her mother, Marioara Pinca, came from a small rural village called Cergaul Mic. I remember visiting the community once in the mid

1990's with Adriana and her mother, and even at that time the village remained very much untouched by the passage of time. It had no electricity or running water and villagers still cooked on woodstoves and worked the land for a living. Her father, Petru Sas, came from a small community called Cucerdea, a place I vaguely remember passing while traveling across Romania by bus with Adriana several years later. In many ways Adriana's past was not too different from my own, in the sense that we were both first-generation urbanites whose parents migrated to urban centers leaving behind the simpler rural lifestyle.

One of my most favourite memories of Adriana's hometown was the evening of November 1, 1994. It was All Saints Day, a time when Romanians visit the gravesites of loved ones and light candles in their memory. Romania has this wonderful tradition of honouring saints throughout the year, a tradition that is so steadfast that even years of communism could not eradicate. As we walked from the small village of Custelnic to Tarnaveni on our way to pay respects at her father's grave, we looked from the base of the valley to the hillside Cimitir Romanesc (Romanian Cemetery) about three kilometers in the distance, just down the hill from the Hotel Trei Brazi, and could observe in the twilight thousands of tiny candles burning as a multitude of mourners made the short pilgrimage to the gravesites of their loved ones.

Bringing Adriana home to meet my family was a very special time for me. It was one of those uniquely perfect experiences when you wish you could just stop time and hold on to the moment for a while longer – as we sat in the living room side by side on the couch talking to everyone. However, it had been a long day for both of us, and after a few short hours Adriana retired for the night. I showed her to her room and returned to the downstairs living room to continue my conversation with my parents. While she was upstairs preparing for the night, my mother asked me if Adriana and I were dating or if we were just good friends. The question was fair, since it seemed more often than not most of the girls that I associated with in the past ended up being more of a friend than a girlfriend. I think it was at that point that I realized that, "Yes she was my girlfriend!" I didn't give much of an answer to the question; however, as the week passed people soon realized that we were dating! My family adored her. My Mom told people that I could not have found a nicer and more beautiful young girl, even had she gone out and found someone for me herself. I went upstairs to say goodnight to Adriana before she went to bed. Standing in the main hallway on the yellow shag carpet in front of the mirrors at the top of the stairs, we kissed. Our lips and bodies pressed into each other. Somehow at that moment we must have been seen by my ever-so-curious thirteen-year-old sister Nancy, who told me years later that she can remember Adriana and me standing at the top of the stairs that night with our arms around each other embraced in a passionate kiss. Her kiss, our embrace, the feel of her body against mine and the closeness we were sharing were still all so brand new, embodied in an aura of excitement, anticipation and a certain awkwardness, as we each began discovering the mysteries held within each other's heart. As we stood at the top of the stairs seemingly spellbound in each other's embrace, Adriana made an odd comment that seemed strange at the time, but became clear as I came to know her. As we held each other and kissed she pulled back a little and said, "This is so weird." I didn't know what she meant at the time. I thought for a second that she didn't like the way I was kissing her. I realized years later that she found it odd that we had moved so fast. Only a few weeks previous we had gone on our first date, and now here we were together in my parents' house feeling like we were home, and there was no other place on earth we were supposed to be.

Chapter 12

Seven Days and Eight Nights

We did a lot of fun things that week. We went cross-country skiing one day, down the trails behind Mississauga Avenue – the very same trails where I spent a good deal of my childhood. It was on those trails that I carried my fishing pole in the warm mid-summer days of my youth, and in the dead cold of winter I traversed those windy, hilly trails on my Dad's old 1971 Elan during my early teenage years. We didn't get too far, as Adriana was somewhat awkward on skis, and didn't feel completely comfortable. Another day we went skating on a natural ice rink on Elliot Lake near the new beach, the same beach that I spent so many summers avoiding as I hated swimming and I burned so easily in the sun. As we skated around the outer perimeter of the rink Adriana held on to my arm, as she was not very stable on skates and sort of awkwardly made her way around the rink with my help. It was a nice feeling as I helped her along. As we skated, two former high school classmates of mine, also home for spring break, were playing a game of one-on-one hockey in the center of the rink.

Later in the week we went to Sudbury with my sister Lynn and her boyfriend, Andre. Lynn was a beautiful girl but always seemed a little sad and withdrawn. Growing up, we spent a lot of time together, due to me failing grade one. As a result, she and I were in the same elementary classrooms together from grade two, when we moved to Temiscaming, Quebec early in the winter of 1973, until we entered grade seven at Westhill Public School in Elliot Lake in the fall of 1978. We had just moved to Elliot Lake from Tesmiscaming in June of that year and found ourselves enrolling at a new school in a new town. Like all resource boomtowns, Elliot Lake was a large, rough-and-tough community that drew a host of people from every culture and economic background. The many contracting jobs in town especially drew in a rough lot of people. When we arrived at our new school, Lynn and I met with the principal together and I requested that we be placed in the same classroom, since we had been together in school since grade two. I remember the principal, Mr. Lane, sitting behind a rather large desk, looking at me with his big friendly face, as he told me that he never places brothers and sisters in the same classroom to avoid students going home and telling on each other. He insisted that we would be fine, and placed us in two separate classrooms. Lynn ended up in Mr. McLeod's classroom and I had a miserable year in Ms. McDonald's. After high school, Lynn worked for a while at a drug store before she completed her RNA training and worked at the hospital as a registered practical nurse. From there she went on to complete a diploma in business administration and worked a while at Revenue Canada before her diagnoses with M.S. While working as an RNA at the hospital, she met Andre who two years later would join the Royal Canadian Mounted Police. They made a nice couple and would be married for almost twenty years before having their first child, Gavin, in 2008. For now though, Andre was driving ambulance and working as an orderly at the hospital in Elliot Lake while living in a basement apartment on the other side of town. During our visit to the Sudbury region that day we met Andre's family in Chelmsford and dropped into a horse stable somewhere nearby.

It was a fun and exciting week. At one point John tried to teach Adriana to drive a car with a standard transmission, but it didn't go over well. The last thing I remember him saying was, "Don't worry, you can't break it." Famous last words as she broke something in his transmission, and as time moved on, it seemed that whenever I brought Adriana home she always managed to break something. It sort of became her trademark!

Another evening we went out to dinner at an Italian restaurant in the Paris Plazas with my sister Kim, her boyfriend, Dean, and another couple who were friends of Kim and Dean. Adriana wore a black sparkly top that evening, and before dinner she asked Kim if she was dressed appropriately for the restaurant. After the conversation, I heard Kim say to my other sister, Nancy, "I like her, she's cute." Kim was always a difficult person to impress, and very straightforward. In time, she graduated with both a degree and diploma, taught English in Japan and eventually settled in Elliot Lake with her husband Rob. She suffered the realization of not becoming a mother to her own children, but years later went on to become a teacher for children with disabilities, before accepting a grade three teaching position at Central Public School in Elliot Lake. Nancy, on the other hand, was my youngest sister and I am sure she has never said a mean word to anyone, although, due to an equal portion of my gullibility and her good wit, she has snared me in a number of humorous pranks over the years. I used to carry her a lot as a baby, and I missed her when I left home to go to school. I remember when I was eleven years old we shared a room together in the hospital. I was admitted to have my tonsils out, and she was admitted at the same time due to an illness. The night before my operation she cried all evening, so the nurses had me walk her up and down the hallway for about two hours before she finally fell asleep. The next day after I retuned from my operation, the nurses told me that she stood in her crib and watched me for a long time until I finally became conscious. That winter when I first brought Adriana home, Nancy was still thirteen – about to turn fourteen in only a few weeks. At the time I remember thinking how grown up she had become, but looking back it is hard to believe how young she still was. Her teenage years were spent at home with Mom and Dad. She had quit school because of an anxiety disorder that no one seemed to really understand. However, she went on to finish her schooling and became an independent young woman with a solid job at Cambrian College and her own home in Sudbury.

During the course of our evening out I learned a great deal more about my new girlfriend through questions asked by others around the table. One question I specifically remember someone asking her was about what part of Romania she came from. Her response to the question was short and simple as she replied, "You would not know even if I told you." However, this got me a little curious, so I waited until we were alone to ask her about where she came from and her response shocked me. I recalled her conversation with my dad from earlier in the week when she showed him on the map the name of the town that she was from, but did not really pay much attention to where the town was located in Romania. When I asked her to tell me what part of Romania she was from, I was half expecting to hear a Romanian name that would be difficult to pronounce and have little meaning to me, other than knowing that it was the birthplace of someone that I was coming to love and admire so much. When she told me that she came from Transylvania, she was shocked that I knew of this place. I told her that everyone knows of Transylvania since it is the home of Bram Stoker's Count Dracula, a fictional Gothic character. Until informed by Adriana, I did not realize that Stoker based the character of Dracula loosely on the 15th century Transylvanian-born Vlad III of Wallachia, or otherwise known as "Vlad the Impaler." In talking to Adrienne I learned that Romanians considered this man to be a national hero because he defended Transylvania against the Ottoman Empire. In his defense of Transylvania, he is credited with impaling as many as 100,000 Ottoman Muslims, as well as killing up to 40,000 European civilians whom he regarded as political rivals, criminals, or simply persons he regarded as useless to humanity. To understand such a man as a national hero, one only has to consider a more savage period when Transylvania was at the crossroads of great empires, at a time in human history when the treatment of those who were conquered was ruthless. Over time Transylvania changed hands from the Roman Empire to the east to the Ottoman Empire to the south and to the Austria- Hungarian Empire to the north – a political trend that continued up to the end of World War II as Transylvania shifted hands back and forth between Hungary and Romania. Even in the post-war years Transylvania under Romanian authority paid tribute to the great Soviet Empire to the east. It is a place that consistently struggled against the intrusion of its neighbours, and the faces of its people seem to bear the markings of their conquers over the past thousand years. That, in some ways, explained the almost oriental look in Adriana's closed eyes, which may well have crossed the vast distance between Transylvania and the far east by way of the Ottoman empire over five hundred years ago, or even earlier as Genghis Khan made his march into Europe. Since desperate times can so often lead to acts of desperation, in many ways one can almost understand how a people from a land that was so often overrun by foreign intruders could find refuge in the ruthlessness of a great leader that stood in the face of transgressions against his people. In many ways he was no less brutal that the defenders of the British Empire who would hang, draw and quarter traitors as recently as a century and half ago.

However, the history of Transylvania is so much more than a simple struggle for existence. It is a beautiful and mysterious landscape that encompasses the Carpathian Mountains to the south and east and the Apuseni Mountains to the west, with it plateaus, valleys, and rivers. It is a land where roads are still traversed by wandering gypsies traveling by horse and wagon, peasants moving hay and other crops by oxen sharing the winding narrow roads with modern cars and trucks as they make their way though the ancient towns and villages, passing a combination of modern buildings and medieval Gothic architecture scattered across the landscape. In so many ways the landscape, architecture, and even the people were almost untouched by time as they held onto an almost ancient mindset in the face of a modernizing world, where magic and mystery are still so real. In so many ways Adriana's homeland seemed to captivate my imagination as an ancient place of folklore and mystery. Somehow, this young woman who I so deeply fell in love with seemed to embody many of these same traits that I found so captivating, and yet she was still in so many ways invitingly mysterious to me. Until I actually met Adriana I did not internalize that Transylvania was even a real geographical place in today's modern world. I had always sort of regarded it in the same light as Camelot, a mystical and magical place, the birthplace of that captivating ancient Gothic look and folklore that I was so drawn to. In many ways, it was that look and image that Adriana seemed to somehow capture and radiate without even trying. Years later, as Adriana and I traveled by passenger train trough the Carpathian Mountains and into the heart of Transylvania I was amazed by its ancient medieval towns, its Gothic architecture and of course by castle Bran, the acclaimed 15th century home of Vlad the Impaler. I was deeply drawn to Adriana at the thought of her lineage arising out of this ancient Gothic world, where the lines between myth and reality seemed almost to fade and merge in an odd combination of fact and fiction.

One of the highlights of our week in Elliot Lake was introducing Adriana to my best friend Nelson, who only eighteen months later stood beside me as my best man, as I watched Adriana walk down the aisle to commit our lives to each other. As Adriana and I walked down Dieppe Avenue and onto Hillside Drive on our way to the mall to meet Nelson, I could not stop looking at her and I think it was making her feel a little uncomfortable. She was wearing a long black wool winter overcoat. She looked so beautiful as we walked down the street in the cool winter air. The falling snow seemed to sparkle and dance around us, and Adriana's face seemed to almost glow in the mist of the cool crisp snowflakes that appeared to come alive as they floated around her. She glanced over and noticed me looking at her. I just could not take my eyes off her. She was so beautiful and I could not believe that she was with me. When we arrived at the mall, we met Nelson. He was only a month away from joining the air force. We were so young.

Nelson and I had been friends since grade seven and were on the verge of moving out into the world in very different directions. From the mall, we walked over to the Royal Canadian Legion where we spent the evening ordering pitchers of beer and playing pool, as we tried to avoid being hustled by two scruffy gentlemen looking to scrounge a few free drinks from the pool table. Half way through the night, as I stood beside the pool table with a pool cue in my hand, Adriana leaned over the seat of the booth behind me, kissed me and said that what I told her a week ago was how she also felt. This was the first time that she told me that she loved me. After only dating for a few weeks, we found ourselves at a point in our relationship where neither of us could think of not being with each other. Looking back, it is odd how we came together so quickly, and in some strange way we seemed to merge together at a point in our lives when we really needed each other. We were young and in love!!! It felt great and we never wanted it to end!!! As the years went by we have had our difficulties and periods of adjustment, but through everything we have loved spending time together; we loved being together and we could never think of living without each other.

It was during this week at home that we agreed to go steady. We were lying on the couch late one evening after everyone else went to bed. I was lying on top of Adriana as we kissed. She took my right hand and moved it over her left breast. We spent a long time together on the couch that evening. That was when I asked Adriana to go steady. I knew that there would never be anyone else for me, and I was hoping and very grateful that she felt the same.

Our visit home ended with a trip to Sault Ste. Marie. Adriana, Mom and I drove Dad to the Plummer Hospital in Sault Ste. Marie for vascular surgery. Dad's health had been declining for a number of years, starting with a heart attack in the late 70's followed by a series of strokes, and now a series of vascular concerns. We awoke early one cold, crisp February morning, and headed for the Sault. In Iron Bridge we stopped at the Three Aces, a Chinese restaurant that we frequented. It became one of the regular stops, as my parents made medical trips to and from the Sault for Dad's checkups and operations. Adriana was tired, and slept in the car, while we went into the restaurant. I remember when we pulled into the parking lot, there was a song by Dan Hill playing on the radio, called, Can't We Try, something about two people being from different worlds. That song always reminded me of Adriana and me, as our backgrounds were so different. As we left Dad at the hospital, and said goodbye I can still see him standing in the hall in his blue pajamas, with his short silvery-grey hair and light blue eyes. He was a tall, well-built man and he never did look as ill as he really was. As we said goodbye, Adriana moved behind me and started to cry. Dad told her that he would be fine, and he was for another seven years, before he finally passed away due to congestive heart failure. He died only a week after our first child was born.

Chapter 13

Return to Waterloo

The next day we caught a Grey Coach bus back to Toronto. It was usually a long dull and boring ride, but this time it went much too quickly. I wanted the trip to take longer, as I enjoyed so much sitting on the bus with Adriana. We talked and held hands as she snuggled into me and we occasionally kissed. We were still learning about each other, so during these conversations we would often ask each other about our childhood. I was particularly curious about what it was like when she was growing up in Romania. I think one of my favourite stories she told me was the time she tried to kill a chicken.

In the part of the country she came from families even in the heart of an urban center still had a small number of livestock, a vineyard, and a garden. As well, just about every household had a pig that the family would feed scraps to as they fattened the animal for a fall slaughter, and most households also had a few chickens and domesticated ducks. Adriana lived at 20 Strada Casnaluui, a small cement block bungalow covered in white stucco with a red high profile tiled roof, situated on a rather large lot that was surrounded by a high metal fence that her father built. I specifically remember her telling me of the roses that climbed the outer walls of the house and the grapevines that covered the patio where her parents, family and friends would sit as they shared a glass of homemade wine or Romanian Tuica, a type of highly potent homemade plum vodka. Her home, along with its urban-slash-rural lifestyle, was typical of most East European homes at the time. Her father and mother built the house across from a factory on the edge of a residential zone shortly after they were married; and thus, even under a communist East European regime, they were considered by law to own the property. Since Adriana's mom worked in the psychiatric ward at the local hospital as a registered nurse and her father worked at the chemical factory as a mechanic, Adriana was often left at home alone during the days when she was not in school, and sometimes even at night. As a child, she always found sleeping alone in the house at night to be a scary experience, but she did not mind the days as much, when she would be left on her own. When her parents were working a day shift, she would often pass the time visiting with her friend Gabbie next door, or her cousin Lily, a young girl her own age, who lived about two kilometers down the road.

One day as Adriana's mom left for work she instructed her to prepare a chicken for dinner. She was about eleven years of age at the time. After she managed to capture one of the birds she cut half way through its neck and was unable to finish the job, leaving the poor bird to run around the yard with its head hanging off to the side. Adriana told me how the factory workers all crowded their faces in the windows of the building across the road to capture a glimpse of this spectacle and hysterically laugh at her as she tried to catch the poor half headless chicken running around her yard. Eventually a neighbour had to come to her aid and finish the job. That was the last time she ever tried to kill a chicken.

During our bus ride back to Toronto I also remember Adriana telling me one story of a time when she was about seven years old, walking home from school. She stopped to call her sister regarding some matter and did not realize that the girls behind her noted the phone number that she was calling. After Adriana hung up the phone the girls called her sister back and informed her that Adriana had been injured in an accident and was on her way home. As Adriana approached her house her sister observed her walking down the street some distance away in her blue school uniform and her white stockings. Mistaking Adriana's white stockings for bandages she was furious with Adriana when she finally arrived home for scaring her so badly. It seemed that her sister looked out for Adriana almost as a second parent as much as an older sister.

We were young and in love and it was such an incredible experience as we stripped back the layers and uncloaked the mystery that surrounded each other. As we continued on the way back to Toronto she confessed that she was afraid to think of me driving my motorbike back and forth from Waterloo to Elliot Lake in the summer, in case I had an accident. I was touched by her care and concern.

It was late when we pulled into Toronto, leaving me with only about five minutes to make my Waterloo connection. Adriana said that she would catch the subway home from there, so that I would not miss my bus and we agreed that we would meet again the following weekend in Waterloo. We kissed and parted ways.

The following week I felt restless and lonesome, after having the pleasure of her company for nine full days the previous week. I was now missing her terribly. I kept myself busy, went to school, and studied late every night. After a few days had passed and I had not heard from Adriana I became concerned, so I called her, only to learn that she had left several messages that week for me and that my roommate John McDonald had not passed them on to me. I assured her that I was studying late and had never received any of them. She told me years later that she was afraid that I was avoiding her in an attempt to breakup with her. However, at the time, with some level of hesitation, she seemed to believe me. She told me about passing her driver's examination. I remember being very impressed that she would attempt such a task in Toronto, with so many streets and cars moving in all directions. Driving in Toronto seemed such a difficult task in itself, without actually learning to drive in that city. In retrospect, I should have planned something special for her. If the tables were turned and it had been I who had just earned my driver's license, Adriana would have purchased a bottle of wine and flowers to celebrate. When I graduated from my Bachelor of Art's program she arrived at the ceremony with a huge bouquet of roses. I think it was the only time that anyone ever gave me roses. Adriana has always been so good about honouring both the small and great undertakings and accomplishments of other people in a way that makes them feel really good and special about their endeavors. This is something that I have tried to learn from her. By the end of the phone conversation, we were getting along quite well as we put behind us the miscommunication. When I hung up, I asked John about the phone messages, and he responded by telling me that he was not an answering machine. I just thought to my self, "What an asshole!"

The week passed slowly. It seemed to go on forever until she returned. It might have actually been two weeks until I saw her again, and I was feeling considerably down at being apart, when one day a card arrived in the mail from Adriana. It had a picture of two bears hugging each other and a verse that read something about a better half. That card lifted my spirits, as I looked forward to the day when we would meet again. Being apart seemed so painful, an agony that should not be endured even by one's most hated and despised enemy.

Saturday finally arrived and I was filled with excitement as I went to the bus stop to meet her. When she stepped down from the bus, it was so good to see and hold her again, and I looked forward to spending the entire day together. We first took Adriana's small suitcase to her friend's house, before spending the rest of the day in each other's company. We went for dinner that evening at Mother's Restaurant on King Street in Waterloo, the same restaurant that had called the police on my friends and me, before asking us to leave the establishment only two years previous when we became a little too robust during the Oktoberfest celebrations. The last time they saw me I was carrying a small Korean man out the door, to prevent him from fighting with just about everyone in the restaurant. Fortunately, enough time had passed that they did not remember me. Sitting across from each other that evening Adriana and I talked about our time together in Elliot Lake, and she invited me to her sister's home for Easter dinner so that I could meet her family. We ordered a bottle of Canadian each and a bowl of French onion soup. I loved the French onion soup at Mother's, as it always came with such a nice thick topping of melted cheese on bread. The cheese was so thick that it was actually hard to break off a piece with a spoon, without taking the entire layer off the top of the bowl in one large scoop. As we sat there that evening and I was admiring my beautiful girlfriend, I noticed that she was having a difficult time with her soup. Lifting her spoon full of cheese to her mouth, she was unable to break it free from the rest of the cheese in the bowl, and just kept spooning the remainder of it into her mouth. After a while, I observed that she had not said a word in almost ten minutes as she sat gently chewing away without making much progress. I looked over at Adriana and said, "You put all the cheese in your mouth at once, didn't you, and now you can't swallow it?" Glancing back at me with a little bit of concern in her eyes, she nodded. I suggested that she go to the washroom instead of choking, but she just shook her head and kept chewing away, almost like she had a huge chunk of bubblegum in her mouth that was just too big to manage. After about five minutes, she finally swallowed the mass of cheese, and then said, "Oh my God, I thought I was going to choke." She never again ordered French onion soup!

After dinner, we walked to the Campus Center, sat next to each other on a couch in the back corner drinking coffee and just sincerely enjoying each other's company. We stayed out late that evening, and as the time came for Adriana to go to her friend's house for the night, I just was not ready to see her off. I really didn't want my evening with her to end. So instead of going to her friend's house, Adriana agreed to stay at my apartment for the night.

When we arrived back at my apartment Adriana called her friend, so that she would not be worried about her. We had the place to ourselves, as John was in bed for the night. We sat on the couch next to each other quietly kissing and holding on to each other in the early hours of the morning. Since Adriana left her suitcase at her friend's place earlier in the day, she had nothing with her except the clothing she was wearing, so when it was time to turn in for the night I gave Adriana an extra pair of my flannel pajamas, a blanket and a pillow and tucked her in on my couch. I offered to sleep on the couch for the night, so that she could sleep in my bedroom with a little more privacy, but she insisted that she did not mind the couch. So I kissed her goodnight and retired to my bedroom. About five minutes later Adriana arrived at my door. I can still see her long slender body standing in the doorway in my slightly too long white and black checkered flannel pajamas. Without saying a word she walked over to my bed and lay beside me. Nothing happened, and it was not until many years later that she told me that she thought it was too soon. At the time it did not matter. It was just so nice to hold her, as our flesh touched without the barriers of cloth. We held each other and kissed most of the night, as we seemed to merge and sink into the warmth of each other's body. We were up most of the night and by the next morning we were exhausted from such little sleep.

Early the next morning she returned to Toronto to work an evening shift at the hospital. Since leaving nursing school she was still living on residence at Seneca College and working as a student nurse at Sunnybrook Hospitals in Toronto. We took a city bus to her friend's house to collect her suitcase, and then walked the four blocks to the Grey Coach station in downtown Kitchener, where we sat together holding hands and talking. Adriana and I both commented on also being very tired. We kissed, and parted for another week or two. Later that evening John noted that he heard a girl's voice in the night, and thought that perhaps the landlord's girlfriend was back in town. I did not comment.

CHAPTER 14

Meeting Her Family

Part of the excitement of two people coming together for the first time is getting to know each other. As they move closer together they provide each other with what can only be explained as a partially-completed puzzle of a multilayered self-portrait. It often depicts the individual's self-perception in a way that shares as little or as much as the person is comfortable and willing to share. Often those initial puzzles are arranged and assembled in an odd combination of partly put-together sections, with scattered pieces lying about that may or may not even fit into the larger picture. These are puzzles with such scope and depth that they can never really be completed, even over a lifetime. But over time, many of them begin to come together and form a deeper picture. No matter at what point in life you find yourself, if you look too closely there are always some of those odd pieces missing, or a few pieces that seem to be assembled into the wrong place; yet when you stand back, those odd pieces seem to blend into the larger picture – and sometimes those pieces come together in a most unexpected manner, finally making sense of something that was previously unclear.

Part of the excitement of meeting and falling in love is getting to know and understand that new special person in your life. It is a time when you first start to become familiar with each other's family and friends and start to ask each other questions. Even the smallest and seemingly insignificant piece of trivia can seem wonderful and exciting. As you become closer and more comfortable with each other, those questions often become more personal, though always respecting what the other is willing to share at that point in the relationship. By meeting family and friends and from deep, private, personal conversations that can make you smile, laugh and cry, you begin to understand the complexities and dimensions of the person you are coming to know intimately. Through it all you gain a deeper understanding that true love is respectful, patient, understanding, and accepting. This is often something that happens so naturally that at the time you don't stop to realize how truly intimate you are becoming, as you begin to touch each other's heart and soul.

I remember that at that time in our relationship, the days seemed to pass like years when Adriana and I were apart as I awaited to see her again with anticipation and excitement. After our night together we talked on the phone almost every second evening and I passed the time by studying late every night at the university library.

Spring seemed to come early that year. By the time the Easter weekend arrived the weather was beautiful. While I detested the mild damp winters of Waterloo, I loved its spring that much more, with the smell of fresh green grass that seemed to flow in from the countryside, and the colourful array of early spring flowers. I specifically remember the forsythias that were out in yellow bloom by late March. Springtime in Waterloo always seemed so clean, refreshing and new.

Adriana had invited me to have Easter dinner with her family. Since there was no direct bus link, with my motorcycle battery in a small plastic bag, I caught the train early Saturday morning in Waterloo and traveled the short distance across the surrounding farmland to Brampton. When I stored my motorbike for the winter at Uncle Herman's house, I brought my battery home with me so I could keep it warm for the winter. Once in Brampton, my plan was to catch the bus to Orangeville, but had no idea where the bus station was located. When I stepped out of the train station I was directed down the road about a five-minute walk to the bus stop, where I caught the bus just before it pulled out. During my brief wait, some Jehovah Witnesses approached me in an effort to sell me a Watch Tower magazine. I respectfully told them that I was declining their offer in the memory of Sarah, a childhood friend who died at the age of twelve years because her parents refused to provide her with a blood transfer.

Once in Orangeville, I walked to Uncle Herman's house with my motorcycle battery in hand. I was staying that weekend with Uncle Herman, and was sleeping in the spare room in the basement. It was the very same room that I had slept in only six months earlier, the day when Adriana and I first met. It was hard to believe how close we had become in the past six months. My time with her was magical. It was a time that I would cherish and consistently reflect on throughout my life.

Adriana met me at Uncle Herman's that day. She was wearing a white dress with black dots, and looked stunning. I pulled my motorbike out of storage and had great difficulty starting it. The battery was dead, so I pushed the bike up and rode it down the hill beside Uncle Herman's house, popping the clutch many times before the engine finally fired up and I had my bike running. One of the neighbours saw me having difficulty, could tell that I was from out of town due to my university jacket and offered to store the bike at his house if I could not get it going.

Later that afternoon Adriana and I went for a walk and our conversation touched on our last date in a nice way. We were both a little shy about what almost happened. We held each other's hand and were just happy to be close to each other. We were engulfed in an aura of youthful innocence in the freshness of a bright spring afternoon – a time when the world was still so new and mysterious to us, in such odd combinations of excitement and awkwardness with what was to come. As we strolled down the road hand in hand I would glance over from time to time and smile awkwardly. It was a time when we would just stop and kiss with no regard for onlookers. As we held each other's hand that day we knew that we were in the last days of our innocence as we began to embrace and discover each other.

Later that day an elderly and very religious couple, somehow related to Caroline's mother, stopped in for a visit. Adriana and I were instructed by Caroline in no uncertain terms to not hold hands or show any sign of affection that might offend her relatives. Sanford, on the other hand, made it very clear to me that the couple were financially very well off. They drove a pale gold Lincoln Continental, and according to cousin Sanford were millionaires who were too frugal to purchase a truly classy vehicle. The elderly gentleman was short, stocky, and somewhat over weight. He was quite ill, and from the sounds of it he did not have much time left. His tall, slim wife with her pointy little pruned face sat a respectable distance to the side of him, very prim and proper, sporting her black horn-rimmed glasses and looking very much as if the morality of the world rested on her shoulders. Adriana and I sat off to the side with a somewhat more respectable space separating the two of us, along with Herman, Dorothy and my two cousins. As we all sat in the living room talking and sipping tea, the elderly gentleman fell into tears as his wife explained that her husband held within him some dire secret that was tearing him apart; yet he was unwilling to share it with her before his death. He cracked open Pandora's Box just enough to allow whispers from the past to escape in a way that seemed to tear at his wife's heart. Sometimes the only thing worse than not knowing the truth is the knowledge that there is a truth you are not aware of.

For the most part, Adriana and I sat quietly and seemed to somehow endure the afternoon with the knowledge that we could still catch a few short minutes alone together later. At the time it made little sense to me, but as the years passed by, I did think of that man once in a while, and could only guess at the grave secret that was tearing him apart, and that he could not share even with his wife. It seems that people usually share such dire secrets when the relationship is young and youthful, as Adriana and I were experiencing, or near the end of life, as the elderly couple were experiencing. In some odd way, these are the two times when we feel we have the greatest acceptance, understanding, and forgiveness for each other; yet where there is true love between two people, that acceptance and understanding can come at any time. Over the years I have always hoped that since he burdened his wife with whispers of the past, he had the courage within himself, and the trust in his wife, to put her heart at ease before his body was laid to rest. It is interesting how our thinking changes over the years. At the time the only thing on my mind was catching a few minutes alone with Adriana. After the visitors left, Adriana and I managed to find our way into the basement alone, holding and pressing our thin firm bodies close and tight into each other, as we embraced in a passionate kiss. Our bodies seamlessly molded into each other, as our souls almost seemed to merge and become one. The evening passed uneventfully, before she retuned to her sister's home.

The next day Adriana arrived with her brother-in-law to drive me to their house for an Easter dinner. This was my first time meeting Adriana's family. Her brother-in-law, John, drove a Romanian Dauche, yellow in colour and near to the end of its life. John was a graying man of about 55, and somewhat losing his hair. He had immigrated to Canada many years ago and only returned to Romania to meet and marry a Romanian woman, who by fate happened to be Adriana's sister. He shook my hand as I settled into the back seat alone, while Adriana took a seat in the front beside John.

Once at her family's home, I met her sister, who introduced herself, and then asked me to remove my boots. For the record, I was about to remove my boots, but did not have time before being so instructed. I came to learn that her sister could be quite outspoken, applying very few filters between thought and tongue. The one good thing about Mariana was that I never had to wonder what was really on her mind. In fairness, Adriana's sister was the first person in her family to really accept me. I was not Romanian, and never would be. This caused her family to feel that we should not really be together.

Adriana's mother remained very much in the background during the visit. She did not speak much English then, and seemed to have little interest in communicating with me. I think at the time she was hoping that I would be moving along so that her youngest daughter could go on to meet a nice young Romanian man. However, in time she came to love me as her own son. In addition, she soon learned to speak some English after dating my Uncle Herman for a number of years. They started dating about a year after my Aunt Dorothy died and were together for almost eleven years before Uncle Herman succumbed to lung cancer. I liked to tease Adriana and her mother about that relationship because technically when they were together, Adriana and I became first cousins. I once jokingly tried to explain to Adriana's mother that my marriage with Adriana was legally null and void because of her relationship with my uncle. It is odd how things sometimes work out.

That Easter weekend I also met Adriana's niece and nephew. Her niece, Adriana, named after my Adriana but called "Donna" as to not confuse the situation. She was a sweet, quiet, little girl about seven years of age. Adriana's nephew, Alex was a few years older than Donna, perhaps ten or eleven, and quite taken aback at Adriana dating someone. Adriana was very close to both children and Alex seemed to regard me as moving in on his territory.

We settled in for a grand Easter dinner, starting with soup, followed by a rather large meal, and a lengthy discussion before the evening was complete. I was not aware of Romanian dinner traditions at the time, and at first was not sure if the soup was the only course. Shortly, though, I found myself presented with a seemly endless line of courses delivered to the table. Adriana's mother is a wonderful cook. Throughout the meal she was consistently moving from the kitchen to the table bringing food and plates back and forth. While it seemed that Adriana's mom made most of the food for the meal, it was also obvious that her sister made most of the desserts that followed. Another lovely Romanian tradition is the alcohol that accompanies all meals. I had my first taste of Tuica, a potent Romanian homemade plum vodka shooter, something that takes an acquired taste to truly appreciate. That day I also tasted several glasses of homemade red wine, a trademark of just about any Romanian home that I have visited over the years.

In part the conversation around the table focused on myself and my family, how many brothers and sisters I had, my parents, my post-secondary program, world politics, economic trade relations, and aspects of electrical engineering – to name only a few of the hot topics. In regards to my education, it seemed they were not sure just what to make of a Bachelor of Arts program, because it did not seem to have much to do with engineering; and thus, did not seem to be leading to any form of meaningful employment. In fact, some years later when her brother-in-law tried to get me to convince Donna to attend university, he said, "Talk to her and convince to take anything in university, even if it is something like you studied." One of the few specific comments I recall from the dinner was Mariana informing me that if I were planning on remaining around for a while, I would need to learn Romanian; however, in true Canadian form, I simply stood back and let other people learn to speak English. In all fairness, I did make a real effort to learn at least a little Romanian, but often found my teacher rather agitated with my progress.

Over the course of the evening I listened to some stories about Adriana as she was growing up in Romania, such as the time she had to live in the attic of her house with her mother and father when the Tarnava Mica River overflowed its banks and covered the flood plains that the town of Tarnaveni encroached upon. Adriana recalled to me years later how her family ate soda crackers during her time in the attic, and how, in the wake of the flood, there was a waterline around the inside of the house and up the side of the furnishing, noting the point where the flood crested. Following the flood, her father applied a coat of paint to cover this waterline. We also talked a little bit about religion and the fact that while Adriana and her family were Romanian Orthodox, her parents were actually born Roman Catholic. My East European studies helped to fill in the rest of the story. The communist block nations discouraged any faith such as Roman Catholicism, which had its central leadership located outside of the communist block nations. They encouraged people, if they were to be members of any faith, it should be an orthodox faith that housed its central leadership in the host nation This provided a greater sense of state control over the dominant faith of the people.

Adriana also told me about some of her Easter traditions from Romania. She told me that as a child, boys would come to her house on Easter Sunday and spray her with perfume in exchange for coloured eggs or sweetbread, and if the boy was old enough, even a shot of wine. As well, her mom would colour Easter eggs by wrapping eggs in cheesecloth with leaves stretched over the sides of the eggs and boil them in coloured water. The eggs would come out of the boiling water in different colours, with a leaf imprint on the side. On Sunday morning her family would break the eggs for breakfast, by hitting the ends of the eggs together. Holding an egg, one person would say, "Christ has risen," as you hit the rounded end of the egg into the rounded end of another person's egg. Turning the eggs to the other end, the second person would respond by saying, "It is true, He is risen," as that person hammered his/her egg into the end of another person's egg. The person holding an egg that was not broken was regarded as having a stronger personality, and often it would be considered a tie if both people ended up with only one end of the egg broken. It was a bit of a game to see how many eggs you could break before both ends of your egg actually gave in to the repeated pounding. This is a practice that Adriana and I have continued to honour.

During my time with Adriana's family I discovered that Romanian hospitality is typically very honest and inviting, with lots of laughter and excited conversations. Overall, I had a very wonderful evening and was treated well, but did sense that there was some level of disapproval regarding Adriana dating a Canadian. Although I felt a little out of place, I enjoyed the dinner and the culture that I was being exposed to through the food, the wine and the conversation.

As for the rest of Adriana's family, it was a few years later that I met them on our first visit to Romania. There I met her grandmother, aunts, uncles, cousins and friends. Adriana always spoke so highly of her grandmother, and I was honoured to finally meet her. She was a short stocky woman who lived on a somewhat self-sufficient piece of property in a life style not much different than her ancestors experienced over the past many generations. She lived on a one-hector lot with a vegetable garden, a small cornfield, and a small vineyard. During my visit there one fall she made nine hundred liters of wine from her grapes. She was a good businesswoman, and arranged to sell most of her wine to a man who was preparing for his daughter's wedding. Adriana's grandmother lived in a small clay home with a high profile red tile roof. Her house was only about five hundred square feet, with a dining-living room and a bedroom. She had a little stand-lone cook kitchen off to the side of her house, and her water came from an old well that she would lower a bucket into from a spool, something that I only ever saw in storybooks. She also kept a number of chickens and ducks and had one pig that she would fatten up for the fall harvest. She had no refrigerator, relied on traditional preservative techniques to keep food, cooked on a gas stove, and like most Romanian households, had a small home distillery that I only saw in operation once. She had a government pension equal to forty dollars a month American that she supplemented with her self-sufficient lifestyle. While visiting her husband's grave in 1994, I noticed the first Y-2-K glitch, with her future date of death noted as "19_ _," I remember commenting to Adriana that her grandma did not seem to plan on seeing the new millennium, but she actually did not pass away until the summer of 2001. Adriana and I lived with her grandmother once for three months. I used to love waking up in the morning in her house to the sound of horse-drawn wagons making their way down the road past her little country-village home, and I very much-enjoyed listening to her speak. She was a simple hardworking woman whose words seemed to hold such wisdom. She remains perhaps one of the few people in this world that I truly respect and admire.

As time passed, the more that I came to know and understand Adriana through her friends and family, the more I came to understand and respect this young woman that I fell so deeply in love with. Even though I loved Adriana so very much then, it took many years to actually know her as well as one person can truly appreciate, understand, and love another in the deepest and most meaningful manner possible. In meeting and dinning with her family that day, I discovered a few small pieces of a significantly large and complicated puzzle that I accumulated over the years in order to form a portrait of the body and soul of this young woman who I so captivatingly fell in love with. Over the years as the pieces began to fall together, I discovered some of those pieces were represented in her hidden strength that still to this day amazes me.

After dinner John and Adriana drove me back to Uncle Herman's house. Adriana walked me to the door, we kissed goodnight with plans to meet again the following week in Toronto.

Chapter 15

Toronto

The end of the school year was fast approaching, with final exams only a few weeks away. I began preparing for many grueling hours of studying and knew full well that once the exams started it was going to be a long and lonely two weeks until Adriana and I met again. I had become so used to being with Adriana that I actually dreaded the times when we were apart.

With the onset of final exams fast approaching, I caught the bus to Toronto one Saturday afternoon to spend one last day with Adriana, before I set myself to the task of learning everything that I was suppose to already know, while wishing that I had actually read a few more of the required readings for my courses. Adriana was waiting for me in the downtown Grey Coach bus terminal when I arrived in Toronto that afternoon. It was a seedy place in the heart of Toronto and it seemed to attract a multitude of homeless people who just seemed to have nowhere else to spend their time. I had been through Toronto a few times in the past on my way to and from Waterloo and had actually stayed in the terminal one night when the bus from Sudbury arrived too late, causing me to miss my connection from Toronto to Waterloo. But this was really my first time, since my grade seven Toronto venture with classmates, that I stepped out of the bus terminal and merged into the streets of the city.

Adriana and I hugged and kissed. It was so good to hold her in my arms again embracing her body, as our lips met. At that moment, I casually slipped my wallet into my front pocket as we walked hand in hand, almost leaning into each other, as we emerged from the bus terminal and blended into the multitude of city pedestrians. To me the sidewalks seemed like an expressway, with people coming and going in all directions. We walked around the downtown area holding hands and talking until we arrived at the Easton's Centre. I remember passing an old grey stone church surrounded and overshadowed by tall sleek skyscrapers. The church seemed to be an anomaly, with its ancient architecture holding strong, in the midst of a modern urban sprawl of buildings, streetlights, and pavement. Adriana could tell that I was a little nervous being in Toronto. I was a small town boy who found the move to Waterloo difficult. For me, Toronto, with its streets that seemed to stretch out and merge from all directions at the same time, with no apparent pattern or logic, crawling with a multitude of nameless faces moving in all directions, was simply something that one should avoid as much as possible. We met some friends of Adriana's – a fellow nursing student named Kelly and her boyfriend Paul. They were both Canadian East Indian. We spent the evening together. First we went to one of Adriana's favorite restaurants, a place called Mr. Grump's. I used to tease her that the name of her favourite restaurant was a nice match for her personality. She knew that I was joking off course. We had a nice meal, followed by a few drinks. Since we did not plan on tipping the waitress until the end, she stopped serving us, assuming that she was not being tipped. For the young waitress this proved to be a self-fulfilling prophecy. I think I left her a quarter, just to make a point. Afterwards we went to a bar that Adriana and her friends often visited in the days before we started dating. We danced, drank a little, and kissed a lot.

As the night came to a conclusion, holding hands, we made our way back to the downtown Toronto bus terminal with Paul and Kelly, by way of a number of buses and a subway ride. When I arrived that afternoon I had left a book I was reading in one of the lockers at the downtown terminal. I think it was The Prince by Machiavelli. Paul seemed amazed that I would rent a locker for just a book; however, I was not about to carry it around all evening. Adriana and I kissed good-bye and agreed to meet in Waterloo in two weeks, following my final exam. Adriana was the first girl that I ever really continued to see after a first date, and I could not believe we had been dating for four months. I could not even begin to think of my life without her, and would have shattered to pieces at the thought of losing her.

Chapter 16

Coming of Age

In the midst of my third year final exams I started thinking more about my future with Adriana. I noticed a beautiful diamond ring in a jewelry store for about $1,800, which was about all the money I had to my name. I had decided that I would hold off on the ring, but would talk to Adriana about marriage. With my last exam complete, I took a city bus late one evening across Erb Street and down King Street to the Kitchener Grey Coach terminal to meet Adriana. As the city bus passed the corner of King and Victoria Street, my mind wandered back to five months previous, to that mid-winter evening of our first date. I thought of how we walked that same stretch of road from the Chinese restaurant to the movie theater, side by side, at a time in our relationship before we even held each other's hand. At the time it seemed like we had grown so close together since our first date; yet in retrospect, our relationship was still so young, fragile, and full of mystery, with so much yet to come.

I arrived at the bus terminal a little before Adriana, and waited outside on the platform in the cool evening air. The spring air seemed so refreshing and full of life. It felt so good to be free from the shackles of my final exams, to stand liberated from responsibilities and expectations waiting in that cool spring evening for my beautiful young girlfriend to arrive. In fact, with our relationship about to move in a new direction, that actually was one of the last times that I could refer to her as my girlfriend. While we were not formally engaged until late June of that year, we knew that we were rapidly moving in that direction.

As the Toronto bus pulled up to the platform and the passengers disembarked, I stood back watching as each passenger stepped down, looking for that first glimpse of Adriana. Finally she stepped off the bus; our eyes caught sight of each other, and she smiled as she moved towards me. She was wearing a grey overcoat and looked exhausted. She had worked all day at the hospital and then caught a bus to Waterloo after work. We embraced each other in a long hug and kissed as she congratulated me on completing my third year.

We grabbed her bags from the undercarriage of the bus, and caught a city transit back to the university. Once on the city bus, she leaned into me, as I put my arm around her. As the bus made its way up Weber Street and turned onto University Avenue I remember telling her that she looked so tired, and was feeling badly for her. We got off the bus at the university and walked back to my apartment, which we had to ourselves. John McDonald had completed his final exams a few days before and headed home for the summer. Once in the apartment she removed her gray overcoat, revealing that gorgeous black leather mini skirt that looked so wonderful on her. She then opened her daypack and presented me with a bottle of red wine to celebrate the completion of my third year of university studies. We drank a glass of wine, and slow danced without music, as we kissed and held each other tight.

Moving from the living room to the bedroom, she laid down beside me, my arm around her as she nestled into my shoulder and we felt the warmth of each other's body. I told her that I hoped we would be married, and we started talking about our future, and looked forward to spending the rest of our life together, but decided to wait a little while to be formally engaged. As we lay in bed that night talking, we shared with each other about our past and talked about our hopes for the future. She told me about completing grade twelve in mid-year at the end of semester one, and how she spent the remainder of the school year working at a pizza restaurant and cleaning hotel rooms, as she waited for her grade twelve graduation. She talked to me about how her work experience helped reinforce the fact that she wanted to do something more with her life, such as nursing. She also told me how she loved Mary Brown Chicken, and that she would often purchase a chicken dinner to take to my uncle's house and how my uncle's family would often order pizzas from the restaurant that she worked at simply because they knew that she was making the pizzas. As well, she told me about how she worked in a few factories before starting nursing school. I was impressed with her hard work ethic. I also told her about my first job working at Woolco as a janitor and talked a little about my summer work as a gardener for the town of Elliot Lake. As we were lying in bed that evening talking, I ran my hand down her right thigh and felt a rough area that seemed bruised. I was concerned and asked what happened to her. She told me a story about how she was ill when she was six years old, and the doctor gave her a choice between penicillin by injection or pills. Since she hated taking pills, she opted for the injections. Following this her mother had to chase her around the house each day to catch her and give her the penicillin injections, which her mother did into the same spot on the same leg over the course of the treatment resulting in a muscle deformity on her leg. This was impossible to notice except when we were in bed together. As the night went on we shared deeper and more intimate stories from our past. It was a very special evening in our relationship as we shared both the simple and mundane trivia of our lives, along with some of the deeper and more personal aspects that one can only share with a significant other in a loving and non-judgmental relationship.

After such a deep, meaningful and soul sharing conversation, Adriana had her head on my shoulder when she looked over at me, with her warm and comforting big brown eyes and asked what I did during the two years between the time I graduated from high school and started university. I explained to her that I went straight from my grade thirteen high school graduation in June of 1986 to the University of Waterloo in the fall of 1986. Somewhat puzzled, she looked at me and noted that since I graduated from high school at the age of 18 and I was now going on 24 in the third year of university there seemed to be about two years missing from my life. It was at this point that I realized what she was talking about, and with some embarrassment I explained to her about my learning disability and how I failed both grade one and grade seven; and thus, did not complete high school until I was about to turn twenty one years of age. Growing up, I felt unfairly judged by people and became insecure about the subject. Yet, when I told her, she kissed me and rested her head on my shoulder, and I could sense that she was not judging me but rather accepting me for who I am. She felt the same about me as I felt about her. We were in love and love accepts and understands; it does not cast judgment. Falling asleep nestled into the warmth of each other body, we opened up to each other in so many ways that night as we shared our history and talked with anticipation of a future together. It was a beautiful night that I will never forget.

The next day Adriana's two friends, Kelly and Paul, arrived and we spent the evening together. While in Waterloo I took Paul for a ride on my 500 Shadow and convinced him that he needed to purchase it for $2,000, which was $200 more that I paid for it a few years before. That was the bike that I drove around Elliot Lake on one summer evening, with my friend on the back somewhat intoxicated, with no helmet singing, Born To Be Wild! I was not over the legal limit, but I did drink enough to think what we were doing was all right! We were nuts, and it was a good thing that the police did not see us. Even today, the occasional time when I see that guy, I can't help but smile as I reflect on just how stupid we were! Although I loved my motorbike, I had decided to purchase a new motorbike, because I found the 500 Shadow too small for Adriana and me. I had a much more powerful 750 Virago lined up. With the two of us on it, the old bike just did not have the pick up and go that I needed!

That evening the four of us went out to dinner at a restaurant across from the Town Square. As we stood on the side of the street trying to decide where to eat, the girls, somewhat frustrated at our inability to make a decision, finally told Paul and me to just pick a place. I looked across the road and decided on a quaint little Italian restaurant. It was a quiet, clean little place with red tablecloths and very few customers. Paul and I thought it was a wonderful little restaurant, much to the disappointment of the two girls, who complained throughout the meal that it was too small and too quiet. After dinner we spent the evening at the Bombshelter drinking beer and laughing, before retiring to the apartment for the night. Those were good times when we were carefree and young.

The next day I took Paul for another ride on my motorbike, before he left Waterloo convinced that he needed to purchase it, and only needing to arrange for the required funds. Around mid-noon I drove him to the Kitchener bus stop for his return to Toronto. When I returned to the apartment, I found Adriana's friend Kelly alone. As I walked down the stairs with my bike helmet in my hand, I looked over at Kelly, and asked her where Adriana was. Kelly walked up to me and said, "Adriana went to the store and we're alone." She was getting a little too close, so I moved to the side, laid my leather jacket on the couch and I asked her which direction Adriana headed, so I could go and meet her. I was feeling somewhat uncomfortable at this point when Adriana actually walked into the living room from the kitchen, put her arms around me and said, "I'm here," before kissing me. She had been in the kitchen the whole time listening. I didn't realize it at the time, but I had just passed my first test. Kelly stayed with us for another day before I drove her to the bus station on my 500 Shadow, where she caught a Gray Coach back to Toronto. Adriana and I were finally alone.

Following a recipe she acquired from my mother, Adriana made me a wonderful lasagna meal that evening. She even brought a pan with her to cook it in. She knew that I loved lasagna and it was the first time that she cooked for me. In fact, it was the first time that any girl ever cooked for me. The edges of the lasagna were a little crisp; and yet, I was so impressed with her, especially since she went to the effort of learning how to make my favorite meal. As time went on Adriana became an incredible cook. She took the time to learn how to make both her traditional Romanian dishes such as cabbage rolls, sweetbread, and headcheese that she grew up with, as well as my favorite dishes, such as my mother's lasagna, spaghetti, turkey stuffing, and even lemon meringue pie. She always makes everything from scratch and it always tastes so wonderful.

Later that evening we decided to go for a ride to Orangeville, so her family could see her riding on the back of a motorcycle. Leaving Kitchener we became a little lost and headed towards Stratford for a while before we turned around and found our way to Orangeville. When we finally arrived at her sister's place, we only found her mother. She seemed a little concerned that Adriana and I were spending time alone together in Waterloo, and did not seem to really believe Adriana's story that we were sleeping together but not really doing anything, even though to date the story was fairly accurate. Adrienne's mother eyed me a lot that evening with a protective motherly concern that was a little unsettling, and something that I did not fully understand until years later when I had my own children. The conversation between Adriana and her mother was in Romanian, so I did not understand what was being said in front of me until Adriana told me of the conversation later that evening. It was perhaps just as well that I didn't understand the content of the conversation; however, Adriana's English translation did help me to realize why I was getting a few strange looks from her mother that evening and why she was so insistent on Adriana and me staying the night in Orangeville.

As we sat in the living room with her mother drinking a cup of tea that evening, I noticed a photo album on the coffee table, opened to a black and white picture of Adriana when she was about ten years old. It was a side profile close-up of her face as she sat in a garden somewhere in Romania holding a flower to her lips. She looked so sweet and innocent in the picture. Even now, it is one of my most favourite pictures of Adriana. Beside this picture was a picture of

Adriana's family, and this was the first time I ever saw her father. He was a tall man, almost six feet in height, very stocky, with short silver-white hair. He died from cancer when Adriana was thirteen years old, only a few months after returning to Romania from visiting with his other daughter in Canada. Adrienne always told me that he would have gotten along really well with my own father, since they both liked to smoke and talk about politics. Adriana told me that when she was a little girl she remembered sometimes waking up early in the morning to the sweet smell of corn boiling in the kitchen. When the corn was ripe in the field her father would get out of bed very early and pick a dozen or so ears of corn from the government fields and bring them home without arising suspicion. When she told me this story I commented with surprise that he stole corn, but she assured me that it was not stealing because it was taken from a government field. He would peal the cornhusks off and lay them on top of the corn as it boiled in the water to give it a better taste. This was most likely something that he learned from his own parents, and even to this day I will sometimes do this when cooking corn because I know that it brings back fond memories for Adriana. Waking up as a young girl to the sweet smell of boiling corn in the kitchen is one of those special memories that Adriana held onto of her father all her life. She was her dad's little girl, and he loved her with all of his heart. When Adriana was born, men were not allowed in the maternity wing of the hospital, so he walked over to the hospital grounds and called up to his wife on the third floor to ask about the baby. Adriana's mother had to shout back from the window to tell him the good news that he was a father to a beautiful baby girl! No doubt in traditional Romanian fashion, he likely celebrated the birth of his baby in the company of close friends and family with Tuica, homemade red wine, and some Romanian cigarettes. When he died Adriana was only a month from turning 14 years of age and often told me that she felt that she was in denial in the months following his death. Shortly after her father's passing, Adriana moved forty-five kilometers away from home to attend a boarding school nursing program in Targu Mures. To me it seemed that she left home at such a young age. Perhaps she just needed to get away, and her attendance at the boarding school offered a means of escape. Although he did not have the opportunity to see his little girl mature into a beautiful young woman, I know how proud he would be with her, as she blossomed into a beautiful young woman, a loving and devoted wife, and a caring and loving mother. While I never did meet Mr. Sas, since he died a few years before Adriana arrived in Canada, I did promise him before my marriage that I would always care for, love, and cherish Adriana with all of my heart. Whenever Adriana and I experienced any difficulties in our marriage I always remembered that promise to her father.

As we finished our cup of tea Adriana and her mother seemed to be winding down their short conversation about our current sleeping arrangements in Waterloo. Her mother saw us off as we began our return trip despite the fact that she still seemed very intent on having us stay at the house for the night – even as we were driving out of the yard and making our way down the road.

The chill of the spring night was settling over the countryside as we made our way back to Waterloo. The late evening spring air felt so clean, pure and refreshing, as Adriana held on to me with her arms tight around my waist, and once in a while gave me a little squeeze. She used do that a lot when she sat on the back of my bike over the following years, and it was for that reason that I used to call her, "My main squeeze." She liked my little pet name for her, even though she jokingly would reply once and a while, "I hope that I'm your only squeeze." At least I always thought she was joking when she would make that comment? Riding back to Waterloo that evening, with the rhythm and vibration of the motor moving through our bodies, she rode well on the back of the bike, with her body molding into the back of my body, holding on to me with both arms as we moved and swayed together following the curves and crevasses of the road almost as one with each other and the bike. When we returned to Waterloo we kissed and made love that night for the first time. We embraced each other as our bodies merged together in the warmth and comfort of each other's flesh throughout the night. It was hard to believe that only seven and a half months had passed since that night I first met Adriana on October 8, 1988, and there we were making love and planning on spending the rest of our lives together – such a few short months ago that I walked beside her that first time for a few seconds as we left the Orangeville movie theater together and I wished so much that I could be so much closer to her.

The next day we went for a walk hand in hand and looked at the diamond ring that I had been eyeing for a while. I don't remember much about what it looked like – only that it was a rather impressive ring. However, we agreed that we could wait on getting a ring and later that day I met a friend from school and agreed to purchase his 750 Virago for $3,000. Dad loaned me $2,000 for the purchase to cover me until I was able to sell my 500 Shadow and pay him back.

It was a cool, dreary wet day in late April as I drove my 500 Shadow to the Scotia Bank in the Town Square Mall to withdraw the funds to purchase my new bike. Since it was raining, Adriana decided to stay in the apartment until I returned. On the way to the bank I somehow ended up riding down the road parallel to, and in the centre of a set of CN rail lines. As the rail line turned left off the road, my front wheel became caught in the tracks, sending me over the handlebars and flying down the road. After becoming airborne and somewhat free flying for a few seconds, I found myself crashing into the pavement and rolling side over side as I heard the ticking of my helmet, still strapped tight to my head bouncing and rolling down the road. I got up, and moved my bike over to the side of the road. A man in a white car stopped and bandaged up my hand. It was bleeding a lot, where my little right finger wore through my imitation leather glove and scraped down the road. The man told me that his friend crashed a bike in the same place doing the same thing I was doing. Since then I have learned about two other such accidents with motorbikes on the same stretch of road. For months later I would often wake up in the middle of the night in a cold sweet from the same reoccurring dream that I was rolling down the wet pavement after dropping my bike on the tracks. After my accident, I got back on my bike and drove to the bank to make my withdrawal. While standing at the counter, the bank teller looked at me with concern and asked if I was well. She said that I was as pale as a ghost, and looked as if something was wrong. I explained to her that I had just pulled myself from a bike accident, and was quite shaken up from the experience.

Once I arrived back at my apartment I found Adriana on the phone talking to her sister. She looked up at me and hung the phone up. She could tell that something was wrong. When she learned of the accident she hugged me, and told me how she wished that she could have been with me, so that I would not have gone through the experience alone. I didn't have the heart to tell her that had she been there, I most likely would have died, since in a bike accident the driver usually cushions the fall for the passenger, resulting in serious and often fatal injuries to the driver. After this, Adriana and I walked over to my friend's apartment and we purchased the bike, and as I counted out the money my hand was still dripping blood from the accident. I could hardly hold the money and sign the receipt due to the throbbing pain in my right hand. With my hand in bad shape, I had to leave the bike at my friend's house for a few days, until the swelling and pain went down. I was concerned slightly as I had a timeline to worry about. I needed to travel back to Elliot Lake the following weekend to start my summer employment. In the meantime we went back to my apartment and had a short nap, or sort of, before Adriana took me to the hospital to have my hand looked at by a doctor, only to find out that I suffered from a vertical fracture that was stable and did not need a cast. While in the emergency room I met a nurse that I went to school with, and we talked a little while.

After our visit to the hospital we stopped off at a Greek restaurant that evening to meet Val. This would be our first and final visit with Val, as the two ladies did not seem to get along very well. Afterwards, we went to the Campus Center to purchase two condoms before returning back to my apartment. On our way to my apartment for the night, we dropped by the arts building so that I could introduce Adriana to an elderly evening janitor with whom I had become good friends over my years at Waterloo. He was a German gentleman in his early sixties and had served in the Third Reich as a soldier during Second World War. He was about five foot six inches tall, very sturdily built, with short silver/grey hair and a matching mustache. He would always stop in to see me as I studied during the evening, and I looked forward to my conversations with him. He used to tell me stories about the war. He once told me that he found a Jewish family hiding in a cellar, and how he used to leave them food on the back step once in awhile. I found his stories interesting. I wanted to both introduce him to Adriana and to wish him farewell for the summer. As we met, I forgot about my broken hand, and shook hands with him, only to fall back in great pain with an explanation of my recent accident. We talked a little and said good-bye. I never did see him again, and suspect that he has long since passed on. Adriana and I spent another day in Waterloo before the swelling in my hand went down enough that I could wear a glove for riding again. It was late April and still too cool to even consider riding north without gloves. I was lucky that I broke my throttle hand. Had it been my clutch hand I would not have been able to ride for at least two or three weeks. We spent another wonderful day together before we embarked on our trek north.

It was a magical time, as we walked around the streets of Waterloo holding hands and talking. We had little more than a few dollars between us, and yet looking back we were wealthier than we could have imagined. Adriana taught me a few Romanian phrases, such as "I love you" and "I want to be engaged to you." As we walked down Helene Crescent one afternoon I told Adriana in Romanian that I would like to be engaged to her. I asked her if she understood what I said, and she responded by translating into English my proposal. A young woman working on her front lawn glanced over at Adriana and me with a look of astonishment, as she overheard Adriana translate my Romanian into English by saying, "I want to be engaged to you." From her perspective, it must have seemed as if Adriana had just proposed to me. Later that evening Adriana called her sister to let her know that she was fine and would be heading north with me the following day. While Adriana was on the phone, I took a walk to the store for some groceries, as we had very little food in the house. I remember purchasing some small containers of yogurt, some vegetables and dip. Walking to and from the store in the darkness of the night, breathing in the refreshing spring air I felt so alive. For the first time in my life I was not alone, and it felt so good to be so close to someone. When I returned we covered ourselves in a blanket on the floor in the living room and watched television. One of the shows was a black and white Twilight Zone episode about a doll maker whose dolls all came to life and started killing people. Adriana always loved watching old black and white movies. She enjoyed the simple and innocent plots. Jay Churchill, my landlord, retuned that evening with his girlfriend. He was a recent engineer graduate from Guelph, and was working in the United States on environmental hazardous sites. He heard Adriana and me down stairs and came to see us. He had never met Adriana before and I think he was a little embarrassed when he realized what he was walking in on. He only stayed a few awkward moments before apologizing and retiring to the upper suite for the evening. At some point in the evening we moved over to the bedroom for the rest of the night. We kissed so much that evening that Adriana's chin was a little red by morning from rubbing against my face so much throughout the night, and as the months passed, a slight rash on her chin was usually the trademark of our weekends together.

Chapter 17

Trip home

The next morning we woke late. We never did seem to get much sleep when we were together, and often found ourselves waking rather late in the morning. After breakfast that consisted of coffee, yogurt and a few vegetables, we headed out for a walk. Adriana wanted to get something at the corner store on Erb Street; however, as we left the apartment we met up with Jay in the driveway and started talking. Adriana decided that she would walk over to the store herself, leaving Jay and me to talk. Adriana was wearing blue jeans and the red loose knitted sweater that she gave me for Valentine's Day. It was a little cool out and she did not have any warm clothing with her, so she borrowed some of mine. She looked smashing in my red sweater, with her short dark hair. As she walked down the road, she was smiling and full of life. She always had such a carefree aura of youthful innocence about her. She gave me a quick little kiss on the lips and said she would be right back. As she left, Jay looked at her and half smiled as he commented to me on how he thought she was cute. After Adriana returned, we went out for lunch at the Greek restaurant near the university before heading north that afternoon.

The restaurant was in a little plaza beside the university on University Avenue, along with a mass of other small restaurants. The plaza was a favorite hangout for university students and had a whole mix of restaurants. There was an East Indian restaurant, a Subway Shop, a bar and grill called McGinnis, and a fancy restaurant in the far corner called the Mongolian's Grill, along with a number of smaller establishments. It had just about every kind of food from every part of the world, and we must have dined at each one over the following year, but of them all the Subway Shop and the Greek restaurant were our favorites. As we ate a pita we talked about heading north later that day. We had planned to be in Elliot Lake by now, but had to wait in Waterloo until I could get my swollen, broken hand into a motorcycle glove. Even in the heat of the summer I would not consider bare handed driving. I had been hit on the hand and on other parts of my body enough times from flying road debris that I wouldn't even consider highway driving without gloves, and taking into account the cool temperatures of mid spring, my fingers would have frozen off long before I ever made it home. I had no choice but to wait in Waterloo until I could squeeze my hand into a glove.

I had spent the previous two days soaking my hand in ice to get the swelling down enough to pull on my motorcycle glove with only some discomfort and pain; yet it was near impossible to remove the glove from my hand. After lunch, I walked over to my friend's house alone, started up my new bike, and drove it around a while to get a feel for it before putting Adriana on the back and heading north. I returned to my apartment, where Adriana and I made the final decision to head north. I convinced her to wear running shoes rather than the sandals she had planned on wearing. It was a cool April evening, and it was about to get even cooler as we headed north on Highway 69.

We were dressed in layers to keep warm. I wore my Waterloo leather jacket, and gave Adriana one of my old faded acid wash jean jackets to wear over my red pullover sweater. With the sweater under it, the jacket seemed to fit her just fine. She was incredibly sexy in that jacket. She hopped on the back of my bike and held on to me with her arms around my waist. She seemed to snuggle into my back, giving me an occasional squeeze as we rolled down the highway.

We departed Waterloo a little too late that day. It might have been almost 6 p.m. before we got underway, and in hindsight, perhaps we should have waited until morning to leave, but we were young and not thinking ahead. The ride north was fine until we passed Barrie, sometime after sunset. As the darkness of night fell around us, the cool spring air set in, leaving me unable to drive more than fifty kilometers without stopping to warm my hands. Adriana was fine, since I was shielding her from the wind with my body, and my leather jacket and layers of clothing kept me warm. However, my fingers were another story. My artificial leather gloves had very minimal padding and did very little to protect my fingers from the near-zero temperatures. At the first coffee stop just north of Barrie, I went into the bathroom and managed with a lot of pain to remove my gloves and wrap my fingers in toilet paper for warmth. Doing this gave me enough added insulation that I was able to make almost fifty kilometers per ride before my fingers would start to go numb, and would often ride another twenty kilometers before the pain from the cold forced me to stop. After administering my "toilet paper treatment" and forcing my broken hand back into my glove, I joined Adriana for a cup of warm coffee.

The restaurant was a small roadside "mom'n'pop" truck stop, with small tables covered in red and white plastic checkered tablecloths. We sat across from each other sipping our coffee and talking about how we were going to make it home with my fingers freezing about every fifty kilometers. We decided to continue on, stopping for coffee about every fifty to sixty kilometers to thaw my fingers. As I sat there with Adriana I remember the warmth of the coffee on my lips felt so good after coming in from the frozen bike ride and feeling a little embarrassed at having to keep my right glove on while in the restaurant. My hand was just too swollen from the accident to even consider taking my glove off. If I couldn't get it back on, it would bring an end to our road trip. After this we pulled into small roadside diners regularly, slowly making our way north. At each stop I would sit in the restaurants across from Adriana with my left glove off and my right glove on, drinking coffee with my left hand. I am sure people were wondering what was up with me. At one point I actually had to stop the bike on the side of the road and warm my fingers on the engine block. I held the engine block with open hands, and felt the warmth slowly penetrate through my gloves to warm and sooth my frozen fingers. Finally we pulled into the Voyageur Restaurant near Parry Sound around 11 p.m. We sat in the restaurant and drank coffee as we planned our next move. Parry Sound was the last stop before Sudbury, which was still a two-hour ride away, and we were both frozen by this time. It did not take much for us to decide to stay the night. We booked into a room next door at the Val Karen Motel. Our frozen bodies came together as we lay in bed that night with our flesh merging into one another.

The next morning we remained in bed late, exhausted from the ride and the night that followed. At about 10 a.m. the cleaning lady came in through the back door to find us covered in nothing but a blanket. She told us that she thought the room had been vacated, made her apologies and backed out. After she left Adriana and I laughed.

After some time had passed we checked out and had breakfast at the Voyageur before continuing on our trek north. Both the Voyageur and the Val Karen Hotel are gone now, replaced with an ESSO gas station and a Wendy's / Tim Horton's fast food restaurant. The charm and character of the old establishment is gone, but when we travel that route, we still stop there for a coffee, and somewhere in the shadows if you look hard enough you can still see a young couple on a motorbike pulling off the road on a frozen night, sharing a cup of coffee in the warmth of each other's company and wandering over to the neighboring motel, arm in arm in the chill of the night. Even today when I see a young couple whiz by on a motorbike I can't help but stop and smile, as I fall back into a simpler time before the onset of careers, mortgages, and investments portfolios. It takes me back to a magical time when holding hands, kissing in the rain and riding off in the chill of the night huddled together on a motorbike meant everything. Thinking back we really had nothing but the shirts on our backs and the motorcycle under us; and yet, in some odd way in those times when we had nothing, we seemed to have had everything. We can never go back. As we move through life we assume obligations and responsibilities that we cannot ignore; and yet, we do need to remember that the complexities and materialism of the world we live in fall short of the simpler times when we had nothing but each other. There should always be time for holding hands and kissing in the rain.

As we traveled north we rested at the 69 Truck Stop south of Sudbury and at Pacey's Restaurant near Espanola, two more restaurants that suffered the same fate as our place in Parry Sound, phased out by the onslaught of fast food restaurants and rerouted highways. From Espanola we made our way on to Elliot Lake. I remember looking into the woods on the side of the highway, as we rode along that day and noticing patches of snow still hiding in the shade of the trees.

We pulled into Elliot Lake around 5 p.m. that evening. Mom and Dad were very impressed with my new bike and were very happy to see Adriana and me. As we sat around the kitchen table, Adriana at my side, I retold the story of my bike accident and my broken hand, and Adriana told Mom and Dad of how I tensed up every time I crossed over a railroad track on the trip home. In fact, I still do that today. Both Mom and Adriana seemed to be in competition to tend to my wounds. It was a somewhat awkward and pivotal moment signifying a changing of seasons, as Mom came to look at my hand and Adriana responded by holding it and telling her that I was fine.

Chapter 18

Home

After Adriana helped with the dishes and broke a glass, we went for a walk down Dieppe Avenue before sunset, holding hands. As we neared the park where I played as a child my heart suddenly began to sink as Adriana turned to me and asked if I would like to not go steady with her for the summer. I felt she was telling me that she wanted to breakup. I could not bear the thought of her leaving my life. I stopped, took her by both hands, looked into her eyes and asked her why she did not want to go with me anymore. She explained that she was worried that over the summer I might not want to continue dating her because I may want to see other girls, since we would be so far apart. She was actually trying to give me the opportunity to breakup with her, rather than taking the risk of being surprised and caught off guard later on in the summer, if indeed I was planning on leaving her or cheating on her. I did not realize how self-conscious and insecure she was until then, as I assured her that

I wanted to be with no one other than her, and I did not care how much distance there was between us. It almost seemed to me at the time that she must have been awfully hurt at some point in the past and was looking to shield herself by offering me the opportunity to back out of our current relationship as a way of protecting herself from some possible and unexpected blindside in the near future. In fact it would be many years before I would come to realize and comprehend the depth of the wounds that she was nursing, and how deeply those wounds would one day tear at my heart. However, as the years passed, she came to trust me enough to lower her shield and have faith in our relationship. Standing before each other that early spring evening over twenty years ago, caught in the warmth of her beautiful big brown eyes near swelling in tears, we hugged and kissed on the side of the road, as I assured that I loved her, would always love her and made it clear that there could never be anyone else for me. She was so beautiful; yet on reflection I do not think she really knew just how dazzling she really was, nor how lucky I was to be with someone who was so gorgeously captivating and who loved me so much. It took her many years before she truly believed me, but as time went by she came to learn just how deep and enduring my love was for her.

On the other hand, I never had to question how much she loved me and how devoted she was to me. Ed Haggart, a good friend of mine, many years later, told me that he never knew a wife who so deeply loved her husband and was so devoted, as Adriana was to me. Ed, of Austrian and Scottish ancestry, was a large well built man in his early sixties with light reddish hair. He looked more like John Wayne than John Wayne ever did, and liked very few people. He always had a cigarette in one hand and a stiff rye and coke on the rocks in the other. He was an incredible card player, outspoken and he could voice his opinion on just about everything. He was a perfectionist in everything he did, could fix just about anything, and could read people really well. If someone crossed him, he would sit alone in his bedroom all night, opening and closing a pocketknife until he figured out a way for payback. He was rough and tough and could be a little dangerous. He was someone who you just did not cross. Northern Store employees new to Big Trout Lake were always advised to refrain from playing cards with him, and those that refused to heed the warning often owned him several pay cheques. No one ever relented on a debt owed to Ed. He looked after a remote outpost for Bell Canada in Big Trout Lake, about an hour by air from the nearest road access. He was once accused of being racist, but he assured me that he was not, because he hated every human being equally. Sitting at the table at the Bell Station drinking rye and coke late one evening, he put his arm on the table and said, show me what you got. It was a quick arm wrestle. I didn't really think that I could beat him, and even if I did have a chance, I couldn't bring myself to it. He knew that I didn't try, and several weeks later he gave me the challenge again. He placed his arm on the table and said, "I want you to try this time." We arm wrestled for about ten minutes before we agreed to a stalemate, only after I popped a blood vessel on my bicep where a rather large black dot began to form. There are some things in life that you never want to know, and a stalemate was the only real way out for both of us. As rough and tough as Ed was, he also had a heart of gold and helped many people over the years, including myself. One Christmas, instead of going home to visit his mother, he stayed with me in Dryden at the Comfort Inn, to help me get my vehicle back on the road, so that I could make it home for Christmas. The starter had gone in my little red truck and I was an eighteen-hour drive from home. Without his help, I would have been on a bus that Christmas. That would have been the last time he saw his mother before her death. After my Dad died, I spent a lot of time with Ed, and he died a few years later from cancer, a broken and lonely man living in a dingy smoke-filled hotel room on Highway 17 in Terrace Bay, just east of Thunder Bay. Ed hated people, but he did like Adriana. He often told me just how lucky I was to have such a beautiful and devoted wife and he always respected and admired her for speaking her mind.

Adriana stayed about a week with me, before I drove her back to Toronto. During that week in Elliot Lake, we spent one evening at Peachy's drinking coffee with Dad. It was his favorite thing to do when I was in town. Dad and I would spend many hours at Peachy's drinking coffee and talking about politics, religion, and mining. Another evening we drove the bike up to Mr. Donut at the Hillside Plaza and had coffee with my brother John. He was working there delivering pizzas with his old blue Escort; although we didn't talk much about his transmission. John was good-natured; he did not let things like that bother him. As we sat at a booth drinking coffee and talking with John, people in the restaurant were admiring our motorbike parked outside. It was such a simple and uncomplicated time.

Late one evening we drove down the highway to Roy's Motel and rented a room for the evening. After about two hours in the room, we pushed the motorbike down the driveway, so as to not wake anyone, and rode back to Elliot Lake. Even today when we drive past that roadside motel, we glance over at each other and smile. Sometimes I pretend not to remember, but how could I ever forget. When we arrived back at the house, Dad was still up. We sat at the kitchen table with him for about an hour warming up to a hot cup of tea after a chilly late night ride home, before Adriana went upstairs to bed and I retired to my bedroom downstairs. There was always a warm fresh pot of tea on the stove in Mom and Dad's kitchen.

The week went by too quickly, and I started to work again for Parks & Recreation. I worked every summer for the town of Elliot Lake for $6 an hour tending the community gardens to pay my way through school.

Adi

MOTEL
Parry Sound, Ont.
Michael & Adriana
July 1990

Summer of 1989
Elliot Lake
April 1989

Orangeville, Ontario
July 1989
Attending Wedding

Orangeville
Mike & Adi's
Engagement Party
June 1990
Elliot Lake
August 1989

Elliot Lake Ontario
July 1990

Chi-Cheemaund ferry crossing Georgian Bay from South Bay Mouth, Manitoulin Island to Tobermory on July 7, 1990.

John's
Wedding
Elliot Lake
August
1990
Picture of Adi
in the Fall of 1989
when she received
her Canadian
citizenship.

August 4, 1990

Chapter 19

Week's End

Early Saturday morning we drove to Espanola en-route back to Toronto, and made our traditional stop for coffee at Pacey's Restaurant. From there we took Highway 6 to Manitoulin Island, and on to South Bay Mouth were we caught the ferry across Georgian Bay. We actually missed the ferry, and had to wait around about three hours for the next crossing. We called Mom, and asked that she contact the hospital in Toronto to let them know that Adriana would not make her shift that evening.

We spent the time window shopping in souvenir stores and sitting on the wharf eating ice cream. It was a special time in our life, when we were carefree. Missing our ride simply meant that we could spend more time together enjoying each other's company on a warm spring afternoon. The nice thing about riding a motorbike is that the men working at the ferry would always direct us to the front of the line, so that we would be the first ones on the boat, and the first ones off on the other side. The ferry had special tie downs for motorbikes, and I would often spend about fifteen minutes securing my bike in all directions with rope, so that it would not fall over during transit. Adriana always waited on the side as I completed this task.

The boat moved at a slow peaceful pace that took you back to a simpler, unhurried time. After sharing a lunch in the cafeteria, we spent the rest of the ninety-minute boat ride holding hands as we walked around on the deck. When the ferry reached the other side of the bay Adriana and I went down to the lower deck, untied the motorbike, and mounted, as we waited for docking to complete. During the docking procedure, it was always a little difficult keeping the bike upright, as it moved a little back and forth from the movement of the ship.

From the ferry, we drove on down to Owen Sound, and on to Orangeville. About a one-hour ride from Orangeville, I stopped to fill up with gas. With the chill of an early spring evening setting in, I looked back at Adriana and found myself looking into her tear stained eyes. She was crying as she told me that she could no longer feel her legs. It had become so cold that her legs became numb and painful. That is something that I always admired about Adriana. She is tough. She must have been in discomfort for some time, but did not motion me to stop and kept her discomfort to herself, until I pulled over for gas. About eight years later when our first child was born, she sat in her hospital bed all night in labour, and never once told anyone how much pain she was in until morning. As she sat there on the back of my bike, her tear filled eyes told me what needed to be done next. With only an hour and a half to go, she could go no further, so the decision was made to spend the night in this small town somewhere on Highway 6 just northwest of Orangeville. We found an inexpensive roadside motel in the center of town, turned up the heat, and went to bed as we helped to warm each other after a long frozen ride down a cold highway. The room got so hot that night that I woke up in a blistering sweat, and told Adriana, "I need to turn the heat down. The wax in my ears is starting to melt." The next morning we woke early, had breakfast at a small green restaurant beside the motel, and then drove on to

Orangeville, where Adriana stayed with her sister, and eventually caught a ride into Toronto.

Without staying very long, I headed north again on Highway 69 so that I could be at work the following morning. Somewhere north of Barrie a thunderstorm set in, leaving me in a downpour for the next six hours as I wound my way north to Elliot Lake. It was a long, cold, wet trip home. Between Barrie and Parry Sound I came upon a terrible accident where I saw a small compact car rolled over on the side of the road. The ambulance had just pulled out, leaving a police officer covered in a yellow raincoat directing traffic. As I slowly passed him, he looked at me, and said, "It sure is a wet one, isn't it." I nodded and continued on. We were both soaked. Cold and wet, I stopped at a roadside restaurant just south of Parry Sound and ordered a hot beef sandwich, with the ever fading hope of the rain letting up before I continued on my way north. I made all of the usual stops on that return trip, at the Voyageur Restaurant and the Espanola turnoff. They were lonely stops for me. I missed Adriana. I wondered what she was doing, and wished that she could be with me. Sitting at the Voyageur Restaurant I remembered the evening only a week before when we had pulled off the road frozen and sat in the restaurant trying to decide if we should continue on, or spend the night. As I sat there, I realized just how alone I was without her.

As the sun sank behind the clouds in the western sky, the rain continued to fall during the ride to Sudbury. Throughout the day I often felt a cold chill as the water slid down my helmet, trickled down my neck, and flowed in an almost steady stream under my rain jacket. After Sudbury, I turned west on Highway 17 and headed for Elliot Lake. I could smell the sweetness of the forest in the cool damp air of the night. That sweet smell always reminded me of my grandparents' homestead just east of Matheson, Ontario. Shortly after the Espanola turn off, I met up with someone riding a Harley and followed him into the town of Massey. I could hear the rumble of his engine over my own, as we traveled down that lonely stretch of highway together. Earlier in the day I thought of spending the night to wait out the rain, but decided to continue on my way, in order to make it to work the following morning. When I arrived at work the next day, my supervisor JP was shocked to see me. He was sure that I would not have returned in the rain the pervious day, and was expecting a phone call telling him that I would not be arriving at work.

Chapter 20

One Night In Toronto

It was not long until Adriana and I met again. As it turned out, I had to take the train south to repair my old motorcycle and place it for sale. Dad drove me to Sudbury that day, so that I could catch the train to Toronto. I remember him standing at the train station as I boarded. I felt lonely and a little sad at leaving him, since I knew he would have to return to Elliot Lake alone. I can still see him that sunny Saturday afternoon standing alone in the parking lot of the downtown train station wearing a casual blue shirt and light blue jeans. He was not in the best of health, and I worried about him a lot. I thanked him for driving me to the train, climbed aboard and headed south to meet Adriana.

In preparation for the trip south, I found a booklet on accommodations in Toronto, and was able to locate a one-and-a-half star $25 a night motel on the east side of the city called the White Star Inn. The ride south was exciting, as I was full of anticipation at the thought of meeting Adriana. We only had one evening together, since I needed to travel to Waterloo to get the 500 Shadow that I left parked in my landlord's driveway.

Adriana met me at the train station. We kissed, and boarded an eastbound subway train, followed by a bus. The bus driver was very friendly. We told him that we were looking for the White Star Motel. Although he recalled the name, he was a little unsure of the location. As we drove down the street on the east side, he spotted the motel, and pointed us in the right direction, before moving his bus on down the road.

Adriana surprised me that evening with a sexy black nighty that I looked forward to helping her remove. She was so sweet the way she was shy about letting me see her in the nighty. Standing in the washroom, she sort of peeked around the corner, looked at me and then walked over and hugged me as we started kissing. She looked incredible. We sat on the bed sharing a glass of red wine and kissing each other in the silence of the night. Then suddenly everything turned from a very romantic encounter, to one of concern, as something crashed through the silence of the night in the room next door. At first it sounded as if two men were fighting and we thought at one point they were going to come right through the wall, the way they were yelling and grunting and slamming each other about. However, our concern turned to disgust, as we slowly realized that they in fact were not fighting, and suddenly almost wished in horror that they were actually skirmishing.

They followed their very loud and robust experience by inviting two hookers into the room, and they continued to party throughout the night. Adriana commented to me that the two women next door would not be partying over there, if they knew what those two men were doing to each other only a few minutes before. The black nighty did not come off until much later that night, at a time when we both felt a little safer. In fact at one point we thought of actually getting dressed just incase we had to evacuate the room, but backed down on that plan once the prostitutes arrived next door. The ladies of the night, while also a little loud, did seem to calm down the activities in the neigbouring room to a distasteful yet somewhat less-threatening atmosphere. I didn't know Toronto well in those days, but later learned that staying at a $25 dollar-a-night motel on the east side of town was not the wisest decision that I could have made.

The following day Adriana and I parted ways at the bus station. She needed to return to work, and I needed to collect my bike. Adriana had asked to come with me, so we could spend the day together, and I could drive her back, but I refused. My bike had been in an accident only two weeks before, and I was concerned about its structural integrity. I did not want her on the bike, since I was not sure if it was functioning properly after the accident. If the frame had bent we could have found ourselves in a speed wobble that could easily send us rolling head over heals down the road. Today I would take the bike in for an inspection, but in those days I simply tested it by running it down the highway for about eight hours at high speeds. By the time I arrived home, I was convinced that the bike was still in good shape.

I drove the bike back to Elliot Lake and reopened my conversation with Paul in Toronto about selling it to him. We agreed on a sale price of $2,000 and I told him that I would bring the bike down to him the following weekend. In the meantime, I started replacing the broken parts on it from an old 500 Shadow that my brother and I purchased for parts the year before.

Later that week, Adriana called me with an interesting and somewhat frightening concern. She wanted to let me know that her period was somewhat late and that she was a little worried and thought that I should know. I told her not to lose sleep. She knew that I was totally against any idea of having an abortion, and instead would plan to marry her a little sooner rather than later. Suddenly the idea of using a condom only once in a while did not seem like such a great hit or miss idea; however, by later in the week she called me back to let me know that everything was alright. Nevertheless, we did not seem to learn our lesson very well, and had a few more such concerns over the following year and a half.

When I headed down south the following weekend, the bike looked like it was in new condition. I left Elliot Lake early Saturday morning and took my little 500 Shadow on one final run. As I moved south on Highway 69, the pavement was wet most of the way to Parry Sound as I followed a summer shower, just far enough back to miss the rain. The drive south was pretty, with the jet black wet pavement winding through the forests of Northern Ontario, backed by an almost yellowish skyline as the sunshine filtered through a pale cloud covered sky.

As I came into Toronto, I found Paul's place with surprisingly little effort. I spent the day with him, before meeting up with Adriana. I remember his mother staring at me with her beady little eyes when I walked into the house in my leather jacket holding a motorcycle helmet. She did not seem to appreciate me introducing her little boy to the world of motorcycles.

We took care of business first. Paul handed me a one thousand dollar bill, and ten one hundred dollar bills, and I gave him the ownership. As the exchange was taking place, he asked me how much I would have charged someone who was not a friend, and I responded by saying, "two thousand dollars." I felt he could interpret that however he wanted to. I then put him on the back of the bike, and drove him to a nice parking lot with a Scotia Bank so he could practice driving.

He had very little experience driving. As he practiced around the parking lot, I deposited the two thousand dollars in an instant teller machine. I didn't trust Paul a lot, and wanted the money in the bank as soon as possible. After about fifteen minutes, I drove him back to his house, and then we headed out for the evening.

We got in his parent's van and went to a house party. As we drove down the 401 Highway he was doing about 140 km per hour weaving in and out of traffic as he passed everyone in sight. I remember thinking only two things at the time: that if he drives his new motorbike the way he drives a car he will be dead within a week, and how I would like to skip the house party and go straight to see Adriana.

The party he took me to had a live band playing, and seemed to be a somewhat seedy gathering of dope-heads and punk rockers. I remember thinking how happy I was that I had deposited my money in the bank before arriving at this party, as it just did not seem like a very safe place. I made a point of not really enjoying myself, to encourage him to not stay long, so we could move on to meeting up with Adriana. After about half an hour we left the party and met Adriana at the college. He drove us to a nice hotel that cost $55 per night, where we had a much more pleasant stay than the previous weekend.

The next day Adriana and I again parted ways, as I caught a bus north to Elliot Lake. It would be a few weeks before I would see her again. Once I got home, Adriana called me to let me know that Paul had asked her out for a coffee. I knew Paul well enough to know that he was looking for a little more than just a coffee, so I asked Adriana to stay away from him. I had a few items for the 500 Shadow that I needed to mail to Paul that included cruising pegs, a windshield and a helmet-to-helmet intercom system, so I placed them in a box, along with a note explaining to Paul that the acquisition of my bike did not include my girlfriend as part of the package, and suggested that it would be in his best interest to keep his distance. I don't think Adriana ever knew I sent him that note. There are some things a guy has to do that he just does not tell his girl about; however, I think she may have appreciated the gesture, since she did confide in me many years later that it used to annoy her that I never seemed jealous or concerned that someone might try to take her away from me.

Chapter 21

The Formal Proposal

On June 29, 1989 I borrowed Dad's car to drive to Sudbury to meet Adriana at the airport after her flight from Toronto. I had begun planning to meet her a week in advance when I decided that it was time to purchase a diamond ring. The best I could afford at the time was a $500 ring at People's Jewelers. It was a cute little ring. I had been looking at it for several days before the purchase and actually asked my sister Kim if she would look at it before I made the purchase. She thought it was beautiful, so I returned a few days later and bought it. Of course, after asking Kim for her advice, everyone in my family knew that I was going to ask Adriana to marry me. It was at this time Kim told me that back in February when I first introduced Adriana to my family, Mom thought then that we would be getting engaged.

While purchasing the engagement ring, I was being served by the mother of a girl I worked with at Parks & Recreation. Her daughter was dating a young man named Michael, who also worked with us. The mother had not yet met her daughter's boyfriend, and when I gave her my name and explained that I worked for Parks & Recreation I think she thought that her daughter was about to receive an engagement ring. I looked at the ring a lot after I purchased it. It was small, but I was so proud of it and was so anxious to see it on Adriana's finger.

As I drove to the Sudbury airport that day I turned on the radio and heard the song Stairway to Heaven playing on the a.m. radio dial. It seemed so symbolic that I actually sat in the car at the airport alone so I could hear the end of the song before going to meet Adriana.

When we met we hugged and kissed. It was so good to hear her voice and see her again, to feel her body and to have her lips meet mine. I missed her so much when we were apart that it hurt, so I held onto her and kissed her even more whenever we met. Having Adriana in my life was the best thing that ever happened to me.

We walked back to the car hand in hand. It was an old car with finicky locks. As I was playing with the lock I remember thinking that it was perhaps not such a good idea to lock the door with the engagement ring inside. With some difficulty I unlocked the car and opened the door for her to sit down. I walked around and settled into the driver's side, reached over to the glove box, and took out a small box wrapped in gold paper, and handed it to her. Thinking back, perhaps I should have put a better plan together than simply pulling a ring out of the glove-box and flipping it over to her saying more or less, "What do yha think?" She looked at the small present wrapped in gold paper that I handed her and said, "I know what this is," as she unwrapped and opened the box. When she saw the ring I asked her if she would marry me. She said yes, and put the ring on her finger before kissing me. The first words she said to me afterwards were, "I hope that I can make you happy."

Afterwards, we drove to a near by restaurant and had dinner. As we sat in the restaurant I could not stop looking at her and at the ring that she was wearing. It was less than a year since I first met her, and only five months since we had started dating, and yet

I knew that I could not live without her. She had become the most important and cherished part of my life, and I wanted to spend every moment with her.

After having dinner we drove back to Elliot Lake. About half way up Highway 108 there is a boat launch and I could not pass it without stopping. In a few minutes we would be home, and I would have to share her with my family. We stopped at the boat launch in the cover of a clear night sky, parked behind some trees and kissed for about ten minutes before continuing home. I wanted and needed those few minutes alone with her.

Once we arrived at my home we showed everyone the ring on her finger and everyone but Dad understood that we were engaged. Once Dad realized, he opened up his bottle of Crown Royal that he always had on hand for special occasions, and poured a drink for everyone that consisted of an ounce of Crown Royal, a little ginger ale and a shot of lemon and lime juice. This was his favourite drink and everyone toasted Adriana and me. After this Adriana called her family to tell them the good news. Her sister then spoke to me to offer her congratulations and commented that I move fast.

Adriana spent several days with me in Elliot Lake. It was a wonderful time, and all too short. We of course took an opportunity to spend an evening in the Algo Inn Hotel for several hours. There were so many people around us all the time and we just wanted to be alone for a while. Adriana walked around to the front desk to register, and then met me outside. We then walked around to the upper parking lot, by way of the ramp, and entered the hotel on the second floor. We stayed there several hours under the covers in each other's arms pressing our flesh into each other as we cherished every moment of intimacy that we shared. We longed for the day when we could be together and not have to hide. We wanted to spend every moment together. Throughout that evening we often fell asleep tight in each other's arms, waking to moments of intense intimacy in the darkness and silence of the night. Her flesh pressed against my flesh, her body tight to my body, her lips into my lips as our bodies merged together repeatedly throughout that warm summer evening in levels of passion that seemed to elevate and bring us together as one body. We became as much a part of each other as any two people can, and through the years that followed the closeness and intimacy continued to grow and flourish. Twenty years later we are more in love that we ever were, and share so much more than we ever did.

Later that week Adriana, Dad and I drove to Thessalon to pick strawberries. Adriana wore a pink short-sleeve shirt with an image of a big red strawberry on the chest along with sandals and cut off jean shorts. She looked stunning and her shirt was a good match for her, since pink was her favourite colour and strawberries were her favourite food. In fact she told me that her co-workers at one factory where she worked for a summer job a few years prior to meeting me used to call her "Strawberry," and if I did not really know it then, I sure learned after we were married that pink was her favourite colour. Shortly after our marriage I walked into our new one room bachelor apartment in Toronto to discover that she had just freshly painted the entire apartment in a nice soft pink. I remember at the time thinking that it was an interesting choice of colour for the entire apartment, but we were newly weds, in love and the colour of the apartment walls did not really seem to matter.

As she was working in the field that afternoon picking strawberries, Dad looked at me and told me that I was lucky to find such a nice girl to marry, and commented that it is hard to find a young woman these days who would find so much enjoyment picking strawberries in the field. Dad always admired Adriana, and she thought the world of him. The only disagreement they ever had was over his smoking. She always wanted him to quit cold turkey and even hid his cigarettes once; however, she soon realized that there was no stopping Dad on that issue, and the one thing that no one ever dared do was to hide his smokes. After returning home from the strawberry field that evening Adriana sat at the table with my dad eating a bowl of fresh berries. Afterwards, as she carried the empty dishes to the dishwasher she accidentally let one bowl slip from her hands, and our home was short one more dish. I was thinking at the time that perhaps I should just break a dish before she arrives and save her the trouble. In fairness to Adriana, it was always an accident, and she always felt terrible when she broke something.

Adriana was still a landed immigrant, and I worried a little about her progress towards becoming a Canadian citizen. I was not very aware of the process, and was concerned that she might be denied. In the back of my mind, I thought that if for some reason she was not able to obtain a Canadian citizenship, then at least she could remain in the country once we were married. She did not seem too concerned about the process, but did tell me that she had a book that she and her mother were studying from in order to be able to demonstrate that they understand some of the basic aspects of Canada as a nation. I noted that once she completes this book she most likely would have more knowledge about Canada than most Canadians. The only concern she really had was that her mother's English was very limited, and she was hoping that the judge would be considered of this fact.

Her time in Elliot Lake was too short, but she had to return to work at Sunnybrook Hospital in Toronto, where she was still working as a student nurse. Shortly after my 24th birthday, my bother John and I drove her back to Sudbury in his little blue Escort for her to catch a train back to Toronto. It was the same car she had broken during her visit in February, and it seemed to me that she would break something with every visit home.

It was a dull and somewhat misty day when we drove into Sudbury that morning. As we neared the city we were following a transport trailer on an off ramp. The transport was going a little too fast and almost tipped over as the rear left wheels left the ground on the sharp turn, tilting the trailer on one side a little before it stabilized on all wheels again. I can still remember John saying, "He's going too fast and she's going to tip. I need to see this!" as he hit the gas and got right up behind the transport so we could have a front row seat of the accident that almost happened. I suggested to John as gently as possible that perhaps we could observe the accident without becoming part of it; however, with good fortune, the transport made the turn and we continued on to the train station without incident.

As Adriana boarded the train we kissed good- bye and parted ways with plans to meet in Orangeville in two weeks in order to attend her friend's wedding. The citizenship question was still on the back of my mind, and as the train was pulling out of the station I remember thinking that if for some reason she didn't get her Canadian citizenship we could get married a little earlier and she could stay in the country with me. I always seemed to worry and think of the worst, and as usual my fears were put to rest.

Before returning to Elliot Lake that day, John and I went to a jewelry store to look at diamond rings. In those days it almost seemed that John was following my example, but not doing so well at it. When I was about to graduate from high school, he was asked to leave school by the vice principal; when I purchased my first motorbike, he bought a similar bike a month later, and now that I was engaged he decided to ask Lisa Cyr to marry him. At the time she told him that she was pregnant, and sure enough only fourteen months later they had a beautiful baby boy. That afternoon, as he looked at different diamond rings in the three hundred dollar category the lady helping clarified that John was purchasing an engagement ring, I think because he looked and was so young. Looking at him he just did not seem ready for marriage at that point in his life. When John's response to the question was somewhat vague, the lady holding one of the rings in her right hand sternly told him that if he gives a ring like this to a girl the young lady will automatically assume that he is proposing marriage. John assured her that his intentions were marriage, and we picked out a nice little ring for about three hundred and fifty dollars. John had no money at the time so I purchased the ring on my debit card and cannot remember if he ever did pay me back. At any rate, it was a memorable month. Not many men can say that they purchased two diamond rings for two different women in the same month and that both rings were accepted with wedding plans made and followed through. In fact, thirteen months later, John and Lisa were married only one week after my marriage to Adriana, and their marriage lasted a few years before they each went their own way.

Chapter 22

A Friend's Wedding

It was a long and lonely two weeks with many phone conversations during the evening hours, as we wished our time away until we would meet again. Since I was driving my motorcycle to Orangeville to attend a wedding with Adriana, I decided to send my suit down a week in advance by UPS, and luckily it arrived at her sister's house a few days before I did.

Since the wedding was Saturday afternoon, I left Elliot Lake early Saturday morning and headed down to Orangeville. When I arrived I was a few hours early, so Adriana let me rest in one of the bedrooms for an hour, as I was tired from the trip south. One of the few disadvantages of staying at her sister's house for the weekend was the fact that Adriana and I had to sleep in separate rooms. As I was lying down in the room, Adriana walked in and sat on the floor beside me for a while and talked with me. The bedroom door was partly open and I could see her mother hovering around the partly open door and seeming somewhat concerned that her daughter was in a room alone with a young man.

Later that afternoon we got dressed and attended the wedding with her sister. Since Adriana and I were to be married in less than a year, her sister wanted to see what a Canadian wedding was really like, so that she could start preparations. In fact when Adriana and I were married her sister arranged to pay for half of the wedding herself with the other half coming from my parents. As well, she found a reception hall, arranged for the dinnerware, wine glasses, tables, and balloons as well as the purchase of wine, hard alcohol and beer for an open bar. She personally organized the gathering of a number of Romanian women to cook a traditional Romanian cabbage roll dinner for the almost one hundred and thirty guests at our wedding. At any rate, in the summer of 1989 our own wedding was still a year away as we sat in the United Church that afternoon watching Adriana's friend exchange vows with his bride.

After the wedding we attended the reception, where we ate and danced. As we sat in the reception hall, Adriana asked me if I would consider asking her friend to dance. It was a girl who came to the wedding alone, and Adriana was feeling sorry for her. I declined the suggestion, because I did not know the girl and felt a little uncomfortable asking her to dance. It was a nice reception with the exception of an incredibly corny speech by the bride's father, who, dressed in a black tuxedo, welcomed people who traveled by stagecoach from the west, dog teams from the north and so forth to the wedding. I must admit that four weeks later at my sisters wedding, I did not do much better when I was asked to give a toast to the bride and groom and welcome Andre to the family.

At one point during the reception, Adriana danced with the groom, to the displeasure of the young bride. I can still see the bride catching a glimpse of Adriana and the groom dancing. She walked straight over to them and without missing a step, the groom seamlessly switched from dancing with Adriana to dancing with his new bride. To be honest, I don't think he quite knew just what happened. As the reception came to a close, the young lady that Adriana gave me permission to dance with drove us home.

The next day I stayed with Adriana at her sister's house until late in the afternoon before making the long trip home. Before leaving we walked up and down the road several times holding hands and kissing. At one point we each said at the same time, "I love you." She said that we would have luck because we spoke the same words at the same time. During times like this I would practice the few Romanian phrases that she taught me, such as, "I love you," "My little chicken," "You are beautiful my little flower," and "I want to take a shower with you," along with a number of other short phrases that would allow me to ask for the time of day, count a little, and convey messages such as the desire to know the location of a bus stop, a good restaurant or a washroom. Over the years I actually learned a little more of the language than most people realize and can actually catch the general gist of many conversations.

Leaving her was always so hard. Adriana made me a toasted tuna sandwich with a big slice of a red bell pepper in it for me to eat on the way home, volunteered to have her sister arrange for the payment and shipping of my suit, and made plans with me to meet the following weekend in Parry Sound.

Chapter 23

Parry Sound

Over the next few weeks we talked a lot on the phone. One evening we talked, and Adriana seemed so discontented at the distance between us, that I wanted to get on my bike and drive down to see her. However, it was a weekday, and I knew that I could not make it down and back in time to work the next day. It was 5 p.m. and I actually thought of driving the seven hours to Toronto just to spend a few hours with her, and make it back for the next morning. When reality finally set in, I decided to just go for a long bike ride on my own. I fired up my 750 Virago, and drove north to the end of Highway 108, south to Iron Bridge and back to Elliot Lake. I was too upset to stay home, because I knew that Adriana wanted to see me, and there was very little I could do about it. The whole trip took about three hours and only one deer crossed my path as I wound around the corners and hills that followed the Mississaugi River south to Highway 17. When I retuned home that evening I called Adriana back, and found her feeling much better. We talked about our plans to meet in Parry Sound that coming weekend. It gave both of us something to look forward to.

After work on Friday evening I drove down to Parry Sound, and Adriana caught a bus for the ride north. I had made reservations at the Sherwood Inn, a roadside motel just south of Parry Sound on Highway 69, that has long since vanished from existence as Highway 69 also exited from the map in the wake of the expanding 400 series of highways. I had not shaved in a few days, and was looking a little rough as I pulled into the Voyageur Restaurant just north of the town sometime around 10 p.m. As I walked into the restaurant I found Adriana sitting at a table drinking a cup of coffee. She commented on liking the roughness of my new look as she reached across the table and put her hand on my face to feel the one-week of growth. After eating and having a coffee, we drove south to the Sherwood Inn and booked into our room. The innkeepers were getting concerned, since we arrived late, and they were starting to think that they were the victims of a prank reservation. The inn was in a nice secluded location on the outskirts of town and was owned and operated by an elderly couple. They also ran a small ice-cream store next door, where they made their own ice-cream cones and fudge. Across the highway was a little roadside restaurant. There was a motorcycle rally in town that weekend, but we didn't join. The couple that owned the hotel told me that they used to avoid letting bikers stay at their establishment for a number of years, until they realized that as a general rule they were good customers.

It was so good to see Adriana again. We spent the next two days lost in the passion of a weekend encounter, holding on to and cherishing each passing minute. We slept in the following morning before driving into the town for a boat tour of the area. Adriana wanted to sit on the top deck of the boat so she could feel the warmth of the sun, while I preferred the bottom deck to protect myself from the sun. When she seemed convinced to remain on the top deck, I decided to join her, as I wanted to spend as much time with her as possible. We held hands and kissed once in a while, and just enjoyed each other's company as we took a slow tour of the surrounding islands and shoreline. After sitting on the top deck of the boat without sunscreen, I suffered a severe sunburn to my nose. Adriana didn't realize until then how sensitive my skin was to the sun, and felt a little guilty for insisting that we sit on the top deck of the boat.

After the boat ride, we returned in the late afternoon to our hotel. We had supper at the roadside restaurant across the highway, went for a short walk, and spent the rest of the evening and night in our motel room. It was so good being together, after almost two weeks of separation.

We checked out of our room around noon the next day and drove into Parry Sound to enjoy the day together, before Adriana had to catch the bus south and I headed back north. We had not been as careful that weekend as we should have been, and once again had a somewhat concerning month before knowing that we were still in the clear. As the years passed we realized that for whatever reason we did not have to be as worried about a pregnancy as once thought, and found ourselves extremely lucky several years later to have our two children.

We spent most of that day at the beach. Then we bought some cherries and strawberries and spent some of the afternoon at the Tower Hill Park in the center of town. We sat on the grass eating our berries before attempting to climb an old fire tower that had a spectacular view of the surrounding area. The stairs to the top of the tower were made of a screen-like mesh metal flooring. You could see through each step all the way to the ground. It was at this point that Adriana realized I had a slight fear of heights. I had to stop a few times on the way up, before we finally turned back without reaching the summit. As we climbed part way up the tower that day, I was so scared, and Adriana laughed all the way up and down. She was scared too, but seemed to be comforted by my fear of heights. It was not until about nine years later that we actually reached the top of that tower, when we returned to the park with our very robust two-year-old son. Once we started climbing the tower he was determined to go to the top and we had no choice but to either force him down or let him guide us up. It was at that point that I decided that if a two-year-old boy could do this, well then, so could I! Once at the top, it was worth the effort of over-coming my fears if only for the afternoon, as the three of us stood on the balcony holding hands and looking for miles over the surrounding landscape. It almost seemed as if we could see for ever, as Adriana and I momentarily slipped back in time remembering that day nine years earlier when we were holding on to the last hours of our weekend together in Parry Sound.

Later that afternoon, we took a walk along the docks, looking at boats, and shared an order of fries from a chip stand. She was a little upset with me for only purchasing one- box of fires. Adriana had always been so carefree with her money and I had always been so stingy with mine. In many ways it was a reflection of our upbringing. Adriana grew up under a communist regime where there was lots of currency distributed amongst the people, but few products to purchase other than the essentials of life. I, on the other hand, grew up in a family that had very little money, in an economy that offered everything imaginable for the consumer. My dad only earned five hundred dollars every two weeks to support a family of seven, and half of that money was used to pay the rent for our house. I remember in grade seven, during a growth spurt, my parents were unable to keep me in clothing. For a while I only had a single pare of brown corduroy pants to wear to school for what seemed like months. My mom would wash the pants at night so that I could wear them to school the following morning, and I clearly remember hearing a few lines of ridicule from classmates regarding me wearing the same pair of pants to school every day.

Even though we came from such different backgrounds, over time Adriana and I found a harmony between us. I learned from her to not worry so much about money and to enjoy life, while she learned from me the importance of doing everything in moderation and still saving some money. Twenty years later, as we walked out of our bank after a meeting with our financial advisor Adriana looked at me with tears in her eyes and thanked me for insisting that we save for all those years, and I in turn thanked her for teaching me that money is not everything and showing me how to enjoy life. While it was just a box of fries we were arguing over, it did begin the process of helping us to understand each other's perspective and personal background. We needed this in order to see past our differences in search of a sense of harmony that reflected and honoured our individual values and beliefs within our union.

From the saga of the fry stand we moved on to a small marina restaurant near the docks. We started towards the door, but I decided that I didn't feel comfortable going in. From the looks of the establishment, it catered to the wealthy boat owners who sailed into town, and I felt a little uncomfortable walking in wearing our leather jackets and carrying motorcycle helmets. In hindsight, not going into that restaurant is one of the few regrets that I have in my life. We were young, in love and I should not have cared what people thought. If I had things to do over again, I would have walked in, sat down with Adriana and enjoyed a beautiful meal with a gorgeous young girl. Instead, we drove our motorbike to a small roadside subway shop on the outskirts of town, where we sat at a white and slightly rusty metal patio table that was situated alone in the centre of a dreary, dusty, desolate gravel parking lot, and ordered meatball subs that were wet, soggy and runny. Adriana did not seem impressed! About half way through our meal Adriana gave me some sound advice. She advised me not to order food like this on a first date, as it is just too messy to make a good impression. I looked at her, and noted that I was not planning on having any more first dates, when she looked over at me and simply said, "You never know!" That sure put me in my place. I reviewed in my mind the errors of my ways and tried to think of some way to recover from this self-inflicted calamity. Her words really scared me, since I could not even begin to imagine my life without her. I apologized to her a little later and vowed to myself to never again take her for granted, and to respect her wishes as much as my own. The restaurant and fry issues were put aside, as we prepared to part ways for yet another few weeks.

We drove to the bus stop and purchased a bus ticket for Adriana. It was a small-town dingy little bus stop in the downtown core that looked about as dreary and down as Adriana and I were feeling. The weekend was coming to an end, and we knew it would be another two weeks before we would see each other again. We walked around the downtown area without going too far from the bus stop, arm in arm and at times holding hands and kissing. The time for boarding arrived much sooner than we wanted, even though we were both hoping that the bus would be leaving late, so we could spend more time together as we held onto and cherished every last minute and second of our time together that weekend. We kissed, and parted with plans to meet in Waterloo in two weeks' time. I got on my bike, and made the long lonely ride north to Elliot Lake, hoping for the time to pass quickly, so I could be with Adriana again.

The time I spent with her was so incredible. She was beautiful and I felt so good just being by her side. We talked about our future together, as we continued to learn about each other. We wanted to spend as much time together as possible, and looked forward with anticipation as we waited for our next date. What I shared with Adriana I had never shared with anyone before. Our time together was magical.

Chapter 24

One Weekend in Waterloo

A few weeks later I left Elliot Lake early on a Saturday morning to drive down to Waterloo for a long weekend. Around Parry Sound I pulled over to the side of the road to eat my lunch. I took a sandwich out of my saddlebags, and enjoyed a quick meal sitting on my bike on the side of the road in a light misty rain. As I was about to pull back onto the road, an OPP officer pulled up and motioned me to stop. I had to partly take off my rain suit to access my license, ownership, and insurance papers. I was polite with the officer, yet also a little annoyed, since in the process of proving that I was legally operating my bike I was getting a little wet, and knew that a chill would settle in as I continued on my way. Even though I was a little wet, the drive down was good until I reached Highway 89 when another biker started following me. There was still a light mist falling, not enough to soak me, but still enough to make the road slippery. As I came upon a yellow streetlight, I braked. The gentleman behind me also braked, and went into a slide. He came very close to sideswiping me as he slid on past me and into the intersection. The bike remained upright, as the back wheel fishtailed, until the driver finally gained control of his bike in the middle of the intersection. This was a scary maneuver that I had the misfortune of experiencing myself on two occasions the following year, once alone in Waterloo and once in Toronto with Adriana on the back.

When I pulled into Waterloo later that day, the overcast sky began to clear up as I followed a Grey Coach bus into the Kitchener bus station. Things could not have worked out more perfectly, as that was the bus that Adriana arrived on from Toronto. I parked the bike and met her in the station. We hugged and kissed. It was always so good to hold her and kiss her. We drove to my apartment in Waterloo, as I had a standing agreement with my landlord that I could use it for the summer. After spending some time in the apartment, we went for a late evening walk down Elm Street to a shopping mall and back again. It was a beautiful time, as we walked arm in arm, and at times holding hands under the nighttime sky of Waterloo. It was a time in our life when things were simple, and we were then lost in an era of innocence that we seem to lose as we age. We were together, and at the time that is all that really seemed to matter.

We slept in late on Sunday morning. I was exhausted from the trip south the previous day, aside from the simple fact that Adriana and I seldom got a solid night's sleep when we were together. We left the apartment around 1:30 p.m. and walked to the Town Square for lunch. It was during this walk that we had our first argument. Adriana was a little cranky due to the hot and humid weather. I did not realize until sometime later how much she did not like the humid climate of Southern Ontario. She didn't want to hold my hand, because she was too hot and sweaty, and she started complaining that I never got angry with her. She insisted that there must be things about her that annoyed and upset me. She told me that I should stop being so gentle, kind and understanding with her, and should start treating her a little more sternly. I calmly and compassionately assured her that if I did have any issues I would let her know, and promised gently to try to be more assertive with regard to her in the future, if that was important to her. I didn't understand for many years what she was trying to tell me, and it was years later that she confided that she used to be afraid that I was too good to be real. She was fearful that one day she would wake up and realize that beneath my gentle mannerisms lurked a monster that did not really love her as much as she loved me. While I for the most part was an open book for Adriana, her personal history, on the other hand, remained much of a mystery at that time. However, as the years went by and she came to trust me, she started to share bits and pieces from her past, and the more that I learned about the people in her past, the more I began to understand why she felt and acted the way she did. In time her fears and mistrust gave way, as she came to understand that I was genuine and truly did love her. In fact, years later Adriana told me that in so many ways, she was lost until she met me, and that she learned from me patience, found her faith and discovered the ability to see the best in people. Those few words were perhaps the greatest compliments that anyone ever gave me. I in turn was in many ways so lonely until I met her and remain to this day truly amazed at her ability to forgive people, no matter how badly they may have hurt her. This is a strength deep within her soul that I can only admire without truly understanding. In an odd sort of way, we filled a void in each other's life that so desperately needed filling. The moment seemed to pass, as we spent the day in each other's company and settled in for our last evening together before I had to return to work in Elliot Lake.

The next morning I drove Adriana into Toronto to her student residence. I didn't know how to get there, so she guided me from the back of the motorbike, and gave me clear directions on how to get to Highway 400 North. It was early Monday morning on a long weekend, so there was not much traffic in Toronto as most of the heavy traffic was still north in the cottage country area. I used to meet the lines of traffic going north on Friday or Saturday, as I traveled south, and the reverse as I returned home. My side of the highway was always clear and free, except for the odd screwball who would try to make a short pass as I approached. As I prepared to leave that morning, we kissed good-bye at the door, because the two old women working at the front desk in the student residence would not allow me inside the building. They actually sent me outside, noting that I might spot some young girl coming down the stairs in her bathrobe. Apparently the college became strict about allowing gentlemen to visit the college students, when, a few years previous, some of the young ladies attending the various college programs started earning a little extra money on the side by allowing gentleman callers to visit them in the dormitory. As I drove off that morning, I felt so lonely leaving Adriana, as I started heading north again on that long and lonely ride to Elliot Lake.

Heading north again, the anticipation of meeting her was replaced with such a lonely feeling as the miles increased between us and the two weeks until we were to meet again seemed like an eternity. I returned home, and resumed my summer employment caretaking for the gardens of my hometown. The young girl I worked with helped me to help pass the time. I had known her from high school, and she too was engaged. We spent most of our time talking about each other's fiancées and the excitement and anticipation of preparing to spend our life with someone. For both of us, it was a way of passing the monotony of the days. It was so interesting to listen to her talking about her fiancée, as I knew him well and always regarded him as an asshole, but in her eyes he was really something special. Being able to talk about Adriana to a friend helped to keep her close to me, as I passed the time until our next planned meeting at my sister's wedding in August.

Chapter 25

Lynn's Wedding

Adriana headed north to Sudbury the day before Lynn and André were to be married. It seems so long ago now. As Adriana was heading north, I drove my family east to Sudbury for the rehearsal, which we missed. After a short meeting in Chelmsford and a light reprimand by Lynn, we headed into Sudbury to meet Adriana. Mom and Dad drove in with me. As we walked into the bus station, I saw the back of a very slim brunette in a long gray overcoat, sitting. I could tell it was Adriana as soon as I saw her and walked straight over to her. I remember Mom being impressed that I could pick out Adriana, having seen nothing but her back from across a crowded room. Adriana was gorgeous from all sides; she really stood out. I could have found her anywhere, any time, from any angle. We hugged and gave each other a light kiss on the lips, but chose to hold back the passion that usually encompassed our greetings, since my parents were standing by our side.

We drove back to Chelmsford. Mom and Dad returned to the motel, while Adriana and I joined Lynn and André, along with other members of our two families, at a restaurant not far from André's home. As we sat there, Andre's family explained to me a French tradition. When a younger sibling gets married before an older brother, the older brother has to wear long stocking and dance sometime during the reception. I commented that this is a fine tradition, noted that I am in fact not French, and expressed an interest in observing Andre's older and rather husky brother, who served as an infantry soldier in the Canadian Armed Forces, fulfill this fine tradition! We were having an enjoyable evening, until Lynn became annoyed with me for some reason that has long since been forgotten. Adriana and I got up and returned to the motel, where we shared a room with Mom and Dad. It was a little unfortunate that we left the restaurant so early, since Lynn and André were still picking out who would do the readings in the church the following day, and they wanted me to do one of the readings.

Once back at the motel we tried to meet up with John and his girlfriend – fiancée Lisa, as they had a room at the same place, but the front desk refused to give us the room number because it was too late in the evening for visitors. I think they were concerned that we would start partying and causing a disturbance, so we decided to retire for the night and joined Mom and Dad in their room.

Adriana got into bed with Mom, and I slept with Dad that night. As I slid under the covers I slipped and made a somewhat sarcastic comment about snuggling up with Dad for the night. The return comment from Mom was something along the line of, "Who were you expecting to be snuggling up with?" I think we all knew the answer to that.

The next day Adriana and I sat together in church as Lynn and André exchanged their vows, knowing that in only one year, we would be doing the same. Adriana was wearing a beautiful pink dress, and I was wearing a grey suit that belonged to Uncle Dale. Aunt Sandra gave it to me after his death, since we were both about the same size. The only other suit I ever had was a green three-piece suit that Dad bought for me when I graduated from grade eight.

When I first wore the suit at my graduation, a friend came up and asked me where I got it. I think he was expecting me to say the Salvation Army or that I borrowed it from someone, since people knew that we did not have much money. I looked at him with a straight face and said that my dad had a friend at the funeral home who lent it to me, since the wake was not for another day, and the body it was intended for was still going through final preparations. In fact, my dad was so proud that I was graduating, he spent almost two hundred dollars for the suit, so that I would be dressed as nicely as anyone else at the graduation. As Adriana and I walked into the church that afternoon to watch Lynn and Andre exchange their vows, André asked me to do one of the readings, but I refused, since I had not been given a reasonable warning of that important part of the service. As Adriana and I sat together in church that day it seemed forever to wait until we could start our life together.

Following the ceremony, we met for family pictures. I was so annoyed that Adriana was not allowed to be in the pictures, since the photographer would only allow married couples in the photos. No girlfriends and no fiancées were allowed. The oddity of it all was that he allowed John and Lisa to be in the picture, because he assumed they were married, since they had Lance, Lisa's son from a previous relationship. I was going to refuse to participate in the family photos, and only agreed to after being encouraged not to make a fuss. It is one of my few regrets. To this day I wish I had of just walked out the door, and forced them to make a choice to either include Adriana or not have me in their pictures. I was so insulted. To Adriana's credit, she was all right with this arrangement, or at least she did not make her disappointment and disapproval obvious. Sometimes you need to go with your gut feelings, and that was one of those times.

At the wedding reception Adriana and I sat with André's sister and her boyfriend, talking about our university studies and what we hoped to accomplish after our schooling. I do not think any of the plans discussed ever came to fruition. When it came time for me to toast the bride and groom and to welcome Andre to the family, with a wine glass in one hand, I stood up with a straight face and said, "Andre, I would like to take this opportunity to welcome you to the family, and sincerely thank you for removing Lynn from our household." Lynn was not amused. She looked down, put her left hand over her face a little and just shook her head. Following this, there was some talk about Andre's brother and me fulfilling the tradition of dancing in long stockings, but this was soon put to rest when Andre's brother noted that there was not a single man in the room large and strong enough to get a pair of stocking on him!

Chapter 26

Back to School

Following the wedding, Adriana and I returned to Elliot Lake long enough for me to put my motorbike in storage for the winter and for her to drop another dish on the floor. Then we made our way to Toronto and Waterloo to start our school year. Storing my motorbike was always a whole day ordeal that involved lining the gas take in motor oil, pickling the engine and covering all the exposed metal in Vaseline. As I worked on this project, Adriana helped me a little and spent the rest of the time with my sisters.

That year, Adriana was starting over her second year of the RN program at Seneca College, and I was going into my fourth year as a political science student at the University of Waterloo. In fact, this was Adriana's fourth year in a nursing school program. She completed two years of a four-year program in Romania before immigrating to Canada at the age of sixteen. In Romania at that time, the nursing program was merged with the high school diploma program, so that graduates completed high school with a registered nursing diploma. However, after immigrating to Canada Adriana had to return to high school before entering the nursing program in this country. I always admired her for sticking to want she wanted, even though she had to start over a few times.

Before heading south with Adriana I had quit my job a week early that year, so that I could spend my time with her in Elliot Lake. With the motorbike in storage, we caught a bus back down south together. As we passed the Parry Sound area we were delayed due to a terrible accident. I could tell something was very wrong when I looked out the window, and saw a Volkswagen Van in the ditch on its side. I could also see several older teenagers as white a ghosts standing in the ditch beside a number of motorbikes. As the bus slowly moved along, I saw a motorcycle boot on the road, followed by what looked like the bodies of a young man and woman covered in a blue blanket. It was a chilling reminder of the cruelties of life. I remember thinking at the time that there will be two families receiving some terrible news today. How sad it all seemed. Adriana hugged me, and said that she did not want me driving down on my bike anymore. In a little while it was all forgotten, as we slipped back into our own world.

Once in Toronto, Adriana and I spent the rest of the day together before we caught the late night bus to Waterloo. As we walked around the downtown area Adriana asked me to please not break up with her until after the school year was over, if I should decide not to marry her. I could not even stand to hear the thought or the mention of such an idea. I kissed her, and told her that I would never leave her nor stop loving her.

Adriana was still at residence that year, and like me, her classes did not start until the Tuesday following Labour Day. This actually gave Adriana and me a few days together in Waterloo before she had to return to Toronto for her program. We arrived in Waterloo late that evening and headed to my apartment. It had been a long day of travelling. The following day Adriana and I walked over to a futon store on King Street a little up from the Waterloo Town Square, the place where we met and kissed in the winter rain only seven months previous. I did not want Adriana sleeping on the floor when she came to visit me on the weekends, so I decided to upgrade my bedroom and purchase an actual futon frame for my mattress. Up to this point, my bedroom furnishings consisted of a futon mattress stretched out on the floor on the right side of my little six-by-ten foot basement bedroom with no windows or closet and one door. Across from my bed I had a series of boxes sitting side by side, and some, standing three boxes tall laying sideways for easy access to the interior of the boxes. I used those as my dresser, and actually covered and stuck them together with a wood grain mactac plastic paper. This was the classic impoverished student's furnishing! Adriana and I looked through the store until we found a wooden frame for my mattress. It was a beautiful warm sunny fall day, and since I was too frugal to call a taxi, Adriana and I carried the frame two and a half kilometers back to my basement apartment on 56 Helene Crescent. By the time Adriana and I arrived we were exhausted and decided to go to bed for a while before actually putting the wooden frame together. It was the last time we had to sleep on a mattress with no frame.

That evening, with the new futon frame assembled we laid in bed in the early hours of the morning after spending an evening at the movies and the Bombshelter. Adriana loved dancing so much! We were lying in bed that night holding each other close and listening to the radio, when Pump Up The Jam by the Technotronic started playing. This was and still remains one of Adriana's favourite songs. When it started playing, Adriana jumped out of bed and started dancing. In the darkness of my room lying in bed that evening, I could see by the red light of my clock radio that cast shadows of her image on the wall, the faint silhouette of her tall thin body with its gentle flowing curves dancing and moving to the beat of the music around the sides of my bed. Even today, when I pop on Pump Up the Jam from iTunes she will still start to dance and sway to the beat, as she looks at me with a remembering smile that draws on memories of her and me when we were young.

Adriana stayed with me until the Tuesday morning following Labour Day. We woke early that misty morning, had some toast and a coffee for breakfast and walked hand in hand to the Westmont Mall bus stop, near University Avenue in order for Adriana to catch a city bus to the Gray Coach Terminal enroute to Toronto. It was early in the morning, and she needed to be in class by 9:00 am. Adriana's long, slender, sexy tight twenty-year-old body was covered with an orange short sleeve shirt, my acid-wash jean jacket and tight fitting acid-wash denims, and I was wearing my university jacket and jeans. As usual, Adriana looked incredible. Standing under the shelter of the bus stop in the light mist of the morning, we held each other tight as we kissed and hugged; once again saying good-bye. Standing there that morning I noticed a slight rash on Adriana's chin as we held hands and looked with anticipation to Friday night when she would arrive in Waterloo to spend the weekend with me. With even more anticipation, I looked forward to our wedding only eleven short months away, so that we would not have to leave each other ever again. When the bus arrived, we gave each other one last tight hug and kiss. As she slowly moved away from me our lips separated, as the distance between our bodies increased, then finally the palms of our hands started to slide away from each other as we coveted each moment of contact until finally the tips of our fingers slid beyond each other's reach. Then Adriana turned to step onto the bus. Looking in through the side window I could see Adriana's long, slender, sexy body making her way towards a seat, as she lifted her hand to wave to me.

Adriana and I both had to be in class that day. As usual, I got a list of assignments due for the semester and started to work on the very first day of school. The library was always relatively empty in those early days of the semester, until the panic of mid-term assignments and exams began to set in. However, on that particular day, the library was even more unusually empty, even for early September, since most of my fellow students were attending a free Kim Mitchel concert on campus. The weather changed for the better as the day progressed, and by the time the concert started, it was a cool bright late summer afternoon with three thousand students gathering on the green grass across from the Campus Center to listen to a live Kim Mitchel concert under a cool bright blue sky. Looking back, that was a once-in-a-lifetime opportunity. Want a maroon! It was early in the semester and I had lots of time to get my work started; and yet, there I was hard at work studying, when I should have been enjoying myself.

Chapter 26

A Year Together

We had an incredible year together. Every Friday Adriana traveled to Waterloo to visit me for the weekend, meeting me on the third floor of the Art's Library where I would be waiting for her. As I studied, I would often look out the window in the hopes of catching a glimpse of her as she made her way towards the library. I never did see her. She would just appear before me as I was caught in my studies and it was always such a good feeling to see her. We always hugged and kissed before going out to dinner or a movie. We ate out a lot that year and had a wonderful time together. I always looked forward to every Friday with anticipation, and every Sunday with dread. I hated to say good-bye to her; however, once in a while she would stay until Monday morning and catch an early morning bus back to Toronto. After a weekend together, she often returned to Toronto with a slight rash on her chin! Her marks improved a lot that year, since we studied together all Saturday and most of Sunday, and we took every Friday evening and Saturday evening off to go out.

We would often walk from the Arts Library to the Campus Center hand-in-hand for a coffee break and a few pinball games. The Campus Centre consisted of a large meeting room in the center of the building about the size of a school gymnasium, with a collection of off-orange couches and arm chairs that gave the place an almost 1970's décor. The chairs were arranged in small groupings throughout the center of the room, with couches tucked around the edges of the room in almost semi-secluded groupings. In many ways that great hall was the center of campus life. It was a place where you could purchase a cup of coffee and check ads on a bulletin board, and students were even allowed to sleep on the couches up to a maximum of three consecutive days, in the event of a temporary accommodation issue. There was a Turn-key desk at the front of the great hall with one or two student employees, where coffee was sold on the honour system by dropping a payment of 35cents in a bucket beside the coffee pot. In my four years at Waterloo as an undergraduate, there was only one time that I really needed a coffee and had no money. Letting the Turn-key attendant know, I poured a cup and paid later. Apparently allowing cash-strapped students a needed cup of coffee in time of desperation was one of the reasons for having the honour system. As well, the Turn-key desk took music requests, and loaned out board games for students to play in the building. Around the outer rim of this great meeting hall were a series of smaller rooms, consisting of the university pub with a dance floor called the Bombshelter, a cafeteria, a small meeting room, a video games room beside the Glow Club, and of course, a smoking room.

Adriana and I would often purchase a coffee at the Turn-key Desk and find a semi-secluded area in the room and snuggle up to each other and enjoy it. One evening as we sat there, Adriana laid her head on my lap and fell asleep. Sitting there reading, I too became tired and laid my head on her side and fell asleep. Half asleep, I heard some guy say, "That's so cute, I am getting my camera!" Somewhat cognitive of the comment, Adriana and I sat-up and by the time the young man returned we were awake. I heard him say to one of his friends with disappointment, "I missed the shot!" Before retuning to the library after our break, we always made our way to the game room for a few pinball games, and our favourite one was the Black Knight. We would play a few games and then slowly make our way back to the Arts Library to continue our studies. However, at the end of the day we usually made our way back to the Campus Centre for a few drinks and sometimes some dancing at the Bombshelter, followed by a coffee in the great hall before slowly making our way home to my little basement apartment.

Chapter 28

Twelve Months

One year less a day after Adriana and I first met, I traveled to Orangeville on October 7, 1989 to celebrate Adriana's birthday at her sister's house. Her actual birthday was not until Tuesday October 10, 1989, but her sister decided to celebrate the occasion on the Saturday leading up to her birthday, so people would be available to attend the party. I did not have much money in those days, so I purchased a small silver locket and silver chain for her birthday. I never had anyone to buy jewelry for until that year, and even though I did not have much money to spend, I really enjoyed looking at different pieces of jewelry for Adriana. I remember in the days before her birthday when I purchased the gift, I had looked at an oval silver locket and the heart shaped one that I purchased. It was odd, but when I arrived at Mariana's house, I noticed that Mariana gave Adriana the silver oval locket and chain that I had considered purchasing, and her sister commented to me that she had thought of buying the heart, but decided to give her the oval one, since it was larger. I did not tell her that I almost gave Adriana the oval locket for the same reason, but decided on the heart instead, as it was more symbolic of how I felt about Adriana.

It was only a year before that I had first met Adriana at this very same location – standing in the driveway completely amazed as we exchanged a smile and a polite greeting. Of course that was followed by intense admiration and several hours later we had one brief moment standing side by side on main-street after watching Heartbreak Hotel. A year later we were engaged, and I was spending the weekend at her sister's house, with her, celebrating her twenty-first birthday. Looking back over the year, it was a magical time. It was a year that changed the course of my life; a year that brought me closer to another person than I had ever experienced before in my entire life. It was a year of excitement and adventure. I treasured every moment that I spent with Adriana, and looked forward with anticipation to our marriage, so we could be together, embarking on a journey that would encompass the rest of our life.

Chapter 29

The Strike

November was always a month that I somewhat dreaded. It was the make –or-break part of the semester. It was the month that I had to amalgamate several thousand pages of notes and several hundred references, collected over the previous two months of research, into five essays, each totaling about twenty-five pages, and produced at an average rate of one essay every five days. As well, it was also the month that I had to begin the process of studying for final exams. With eighty percent of my grade point average resting on my essays and final exams, November was really the month that would make or break me.

While November was usually a grueling month, this year something beautiful happened. In early November the Ontario College Teachers' Union went on strike for twenty wonderful days; thus, allowing Adriana and me to spend the entire time together in Waterloo. For the entire period of the strike we spent every day and night together and it was so nice to spend time with her without having to part ways at the conclusion of each weekend. During the strike, we walked to school every morning and she would go to the Arts Library and study for the day while I attended my classes. We met daily for lunch, sometimes at the Bombshelter and other times at the Greek restaurant or the Subway Shop. Between classes, most of our spare time was spent studying together in the Arts Library, with occasional coffee breaks at the Campus Center followed by a few video games just beyond the Glow Club at the back of the Campus Centre. We concluded each afternoon by walking home together hand-in-hand, often stopping at the grocery store to purchase something to cook for supper. After eating, we always returned to the Arts Library and studied until midnight, with at least one half-hour coffee and a few pinball games at the Campus Center before returning home for the night. One afternoon, walking hand in hand to the grocery store Adriana looked at me and said, "This is just like being married. We are together all the time." When she said this to me, I put my arm around her, pulled her a little closer, gave her a kiss on the side of her head, and told her that I loved her. We were so young and innocent at the time, but some things never change, and now over twenty years later we still walk in to the grocery story hand in hand, and will once in a while sneak a little kiss if no one is looking.

Adriana and I worked hard that month and we accomplished our tasks. Her grades improved drastically as a result of the extra effort that she applied to her studies during the strike. In fact, she often told me that overall, her grade point average increased by at least ten percent after she met me, due to the many long hours we would study together in the Arts Library.

About mid-way through the strike, I had to travel to Toronto and spend the day at the legislature as part of my program. My Ontario studies professor rented a van and drove his class of fifteen students to the Ontario Legislature to meet with University of Waterloo political science graduates that were working for the Government of Ontario. He wanted his class to see some of the opportunities that awaited them following the completion of their degree requirements.

It was an interesting afternoon spent meeting with policy advisors and ministerial assistants. One gentleman who talked to us that day was a policy advisor to the Minister of Agriculture.

I remember returning home very tired that afternoon, and found that instead of studying for the day, Adriana dedicated her afternoon to working in the apartment cooking me supper. She made a beautiful Romanian meal that consisted of meatballs, salad and a potato dish cooked up with sour cream, boiled eggs and cheese. She even invited John McDonald to share the meal with us, but he declined because he felt that potatoes should be served plain, without cheese and sour cream. He was always sort of a stick-in-the-mud anyway. Adriana added grated potatoes to the meatballs, and made the mistake of grating the potatoes on the large grater instead of using a fine one. As a result, the meatball mixture did not absorb the potatoes, leaving large grated potatoes visibly mixed in with the ground meat. Had she not told me that she grated the potatoes too large I would not have known that anything was wrong and would have assumed that that was just the way they cooked meatballs in Romania. It was a beautiful meal, and I was so impressed that she took the time to cook for me.

The following day, Adriana had to return to Toronto for the afternoon for a meeting regarding her application for Canadian citizenship, but she had no money, so I lent her my extra debit card. A few months previous I had received a new card and put my old one on the side as an extra. I did not realize at the time that once I activated my new card, the old one was automatically deactivated. Before Adriana left, I gave her my pin number and my extra card, so that she would have enough money to get around Toronto and purchase a return ticket to Waterloo. To her surprise and mine, she called me from Toronto, collect, in a panic, because she discovered that my card was no longer activated and she was in Toronto without even enough money in her pocket for a subway token. I was going to travel into Toronto to help her until she called a friend, whose father and she drove to the Grey Coach terminal and loaned Adriana enough money for subway fare and a return ticket to Waterloo. I felt horrible about this and was afraid that Adriana would be terribly upset with me for leaving her stranded in Toronto with a deactivated bank card and no money. But when Adriana returned, she was in good humor and just happy to have resolved the ordeal and returned to me for the remainder of the week. She took the attitude that I gave her the card in good faith and was not aware that it had been deactivated, so why on Earth should she be upset with me? Anyone else would have been upset, but she was always so sensible in this way.

Throughout the week we continued to study every night until midnight, and watched the news every evening when we returned home to follow the progress of the strike. We were both hoping that it would continue as long as possible, so that we could spend a little more time together. It was just so wonderful spending our days studying together, eating together and sleeping beside each other night after night. We wanted it to continue and never end. But the strike did come to an end, and we once again had to part ways and be content with our weekends of passion and dedicated studying followed by four days of separation, as we waited for the time to come when we could be together as husband and wife for the rest of our life.

Before returning to Toronto, Adriana reminded me to think of her and her mother, as they were about to see a judge to receive their Canadian citizenship that week, and she called me later in the week to let me know that the judge was really nice and both she and her mother were now Canadian citizens. As usual, I did not do anything special for the occasion, and have always regretted not traveling to Toronto for the ceremony. I should have missed my classes and been there with her for that special occasion. If the situation was reversed, Adriana would have been right there beside me and made a big deal out of the occasion in a way that would have made me feel really special. However, over the years I have tried to be better at recognizing special events for her and my family.

Chapter 30

Home for the Holidays

After completing my final exam, and on route to Elliot Lake for the Christmas holiday, Adriana and I met in Toronto during an eight-hour layover before I continued on my way north. When I arrived at the Toronto bus terminal, both Adriana and a friend of mine were waiting for me. As I stepped down from the bus, Adriana and I hugged and kissed before I turned to introduce her to my friend Len Wong who was standing off to the side a little.

Len was a Chinese immigrant student. Like myself, he had very little money and studied very hard. I met him in my first year at the University of Waterloo in an environmental studies class, when he was a fourth year environmental studies student and I was in my freshman year. I admired him a lot for his keen mind, his dedication to hard work, and his good study practices. During my first year of university I had a budget of twenty-five dollars per week for food, laundry, and entertainment. You would not believe how much clothing a person can really fit into a washing machine if you properly balance the load distribution, nor imagine how much food an impoverished student can actually purchase with five dollars at the reduced-to-rot bins! Like Len, I studied six and a half days a week for about twelve hours per day, in addition to attending classes. The half day off occurred every Friday night from 9 pm until midnight, when Len and I would meet for the one dollar movie night on campus and share a pitcher of beer and a bag of potato chips at the Bombshelter after the movie, before returning to another week of studying. Len graduated at the end of my first year and moved on to the University of Toronto, where he earned a master's degree in library science. A few months following my marriage to Adriana, Len invited us to his wedding. We last saw him and his wife about a year after his marriage, after he and his wife had their first child. We kept in touch by writing the odd letter; but over the years I gradually lost contact with him.

Len had never been north of Toronto, and gratefully accepted my invitation to spend some time in Elliot Lake over the Christmas holidays. Although Adriana actually never met Len, she did agree to travel north with him by Grey Coach on Boxing Day. Since they were to be traveling companions, I thought it was best that I introduce her to Len on my way home for the holidays. After meeting in the bus station, the three of us went out to dinner and made our final plans for them to meet and travel to Elliot Lake on December 26. My bus to Sudbury did not leave until 11:30 p.m. that evening, so after dinner Len departed for home, leaving Adriana and me to walk around Toronto hand in hand, window shopping and talking about things that have long since slipped into lost memories, as we slowly made our way back to the bus terminal.

Just before my bus was about to depart, we kissed and parted ways, and I looked forward with anticipation to her and Len arriving in Elliot Lake on Boxing Day. Adriana stood along side the bus and waved as it left the loading platform and merged into the streets of Toronto. Although I had just completed my fall semester exams, Adriana still had to attend classes for a few more days in order to compensate for the time she missed from her program due to the strike.

Chapter 31

Revolution

As we move through life, the one thing that we can always count on is that things never stay the same. We are always evolving. Sometimes changes are subtle, such as the love that can grow and evolve over the years between two people, and at other times changes are rapid, catching you off guard and changing you forever. In those simple days when we first met, we thought we were so in love, but as the years passed and we grew closer together we realized that back when we were dating we were really only starting our journey together. As the years passed the commitment, devotion and love we shared continued to grow and developed so far beyond what we could have ever imagined in those early days of our youth, as we stood together on the threshold of what was to come. Other times life-altering changes come rapidly and grab hold of you in the most unexpected ways – that change you forever. As I kissed Adriana good-bye and boarded the bus that December evening, we could not have imagined the upheaval and changes that were about to grab hold of her homeland. Romania, in one violent and passionate outburst, stood on the eve of emerging into the world from behind the cloak of the Iron Curtain, transforming itself forever. It was the week of December 12, 1989.

From the first time I met Adriana I was attracted to her in so many ways. She was perhaps one of the most gorgeous girls I had ever seen; I loved her accent, and the aura about her that told the world in a most innocent way that she loved life and saw the best in people around her. In so many ways part of my attraction to Adriana was also the mystery of her homeland, hidden and isolated from the world, tucked away behind the Iron Curtain that stretched through Eastern Europe from the Artic Ocean to the Baltic Sea. The secrecy and isolation of the part of the world that she emerged from, in some odd way added to the mystique of this beautiful young woman to whom I was so attracted and was drawn towards by a force within me that I could not control.

Growing up under the blanket of the Cold War, I was always fascinated with stories of heroism as defectors made their escape from behind the Iron Curtain to the west, and marveled at the odd soul who would go the other direction. Adriana was only fourteen when she decided to leave Romania and join her sister in Canada. Her mother did not want to leave her home country, but since Adriana was determined to find her way to Canada, her mother decided to follow her, simply because she did not want to remain alone in Romania while her two daughters were an ocean away in Canada. I found Adriana's story of her escape from Romania interesting, in that it added a new dimension to my perspective of Eastern Europe. Instead of defecting to Canada, she actually immigrated to Canada under humanitarian considerations. Because Adriana's father passed way when she was only thirteen years old, leaving her and her mother alone in Romania, the government officials allowed Adriana and her mother to leave Romania legally in order to move to Canada and live with her only sister. However, her relocation did not go without its snags and struggles. Over a two-year period Adriana and her mother had to dedicate many days standing in long lines at the police station in Tirgu Mures to complete and submit paperwork in order to legally leave the country. This caused Adriana to miss countless days of classes as they patiently waited for permission to immigrate.

To help with the process, they offered the right people American cash, bottles of foreign whisky and cigarettes, as well as packages of dry ground coffee. There were always shortages of luxury items in Romania in those days, as Ceausescu worked diligently to pay off a ten billion dollar national debt it had amassed over many years, by selling national resources and leaving his own countrymen with little beyond the basic essentials of life. In that economic and political culture, a few well-placed bribes went a long way towards greasing the wheels of bureaucracy. After spending a year in long lines at the police station and bribing all the right people, Adriana and her mother received notice in the mail that their request to leave Romania was denied. One of Adriana's most endearing qualities is her stubbornness. If she really wants to do something, she will do it, no matter what anyone says, does, or thinks. While disappointed, the denied permission to leave Romania simply meant that she needed to begin over again the entire process of missing classes to stand in long lines, submitting paperwork and bribing the right public officials. Even after all this work, her second attempt to leave Romania would most likely have also been denied without the assistance of her uncle Ghita. He was a waiter at a classy restaurant in Tirnaveni, and thus had many contacts with high level bureaucrats and police officers. He used those contacts to help Adriana and her mother gain approval for their immigration under humanitarian consideration, in order to reunite them with Mariana following the death of Mr. Sas. However, no one does anything for free, even close family members, and her uncle Ghita, with his own motives for helping Adriana and her mother, was no exception. Mrs. Sas had a beautiful bungalow that she and her husband built when they were first married, and if she gained approval to leave Romania, she was required to sell her home to the government prior to leaving the country, because people living outside of Romania were not permitted to own property in the country. Thus, Mrs. Sas made an agreement with Ghita that his daughter would rent the bungalow from the government once

Mrs. Sas completed the final sale. If Adriana and her mother were not permitted to move to Canada, then Ghita's daughter would not get the house. Hence, he was strongly motivated to influence a few political connections and secure the legal exodus of Adriana and her mother from Romania.

As well, everything done in Romania had to be in secret, since neighbours, friends, and even family were always looking to report people to officials. When her father made a visit to Canada just a few months before he was diagnosed with cancer of the pancreas, the planning and approval of the trip had to be done is such secrecy because anyone, envious of the good fortune of another person, would report the plans to an official who would then work to either kibosh the plans or seek additional bribes for the plans to move ahead. With Adriana and her mother, it was a little different this time, since her father had passed away and they needed the help of close family to get through the bureaucracy. When Adriana and her mother were finally permitted to leave the country they had to sell their home and most of their personal belongings and leave everything behind except for a suitcase of clothing that could accompany them on their travels. In so many ways, it was starting from scratch. Adriana had always wanted to follow her sister to Canada, and it did not matter if she had to leave everything behind, learn a new language, and start over.

Adriana's mother received a letter by mail in mid November of 1984, notifying her that she and Adriana were allowed to move to Canada. After receiving this letter, Adriana continued to go to school until the Christmas break, then withdrew from the program. Before leaving, her classmates presented her with a large shaggy stuffed toy monkey that looked something like a big Teddy Bear, and years later we rescued that monkey from her sister's yard sale. Her mother then began the long and painful process of selling everything they had in Romania, including the home that she had built with her husband where she had raised their two children, and selling all of their personal belonging with the exception of a suitcase and a few articles of clothing.

After almost three months of preparation for the move, Adriana and her mother spent their last day in their house – on February 14th, 1985. Then they caught an evening bus on February 15th accompanied by her uncle Ghita, her aunt Livia, her uncle Alex and her cousin Lili. They took the bus to Medias where they caught an overnight train to Bucharest. Adriana and I made that identical trip in reverse almost ten years later. I remember Medias well. It is an industrial town with a wonderful little pastry shop that had the most beautiful washroom facilities I ever saw in Romania. In Romania such facilities are a real rarity, so you take note of a good find such as this, and may even plan your visit to town around visiting the facility as needed. I am not sure what things are like today, but in those days public washrooms left much to be desired. The one in the Bucharest train station consisted of a row of stalls with holes in the concrete floor, requiring some poor washroom attendant to make her way up and down the row of stalls throwing a bucket of water in each stall, one after another, to wash everything down the hole. Over the years whenever I think I have a difficult job, I often will reflect on that poor lady working the Bucharest train station facilities and take a second sober look at my own good fortune.

On route to Canada, Adriana and her family arrived in Bucharest on the morning of February 16, 1985 and stayed in a hotel the night before catching a flight out of the country. Adriana remembers the hotel as being very cold, since the heating system was not working that well. She and Lily spent her last night in Romania alone in a room, cuddled in a bed and covered in blankets that they scavenged from the other rooms in the hotel in order to stay warm. Being so much younger than her sister and with both of her parents engaged in fulltime employment, in many ways, with the exception of Lili's friendship, Adriana's childhood years were lonely. Being near the same age, the girls were very close growing up and in some ways were more like sisters than cousins. Her first memory of visiting Lily in her home was at the young age of only four years, as she walked to Lily's house holding her mother's hand. Over the years they spent a lot of time together. In fact, the first time Adriana got drunk was when she was only eleven years old, when the two of girls got into her aunt and uncle's alcohol that he kept stored on open glass shelves at the far end of his living room. He always had a lot of alcohol in the house, due to his connections at the restaurant where he was employed. On New Year's Eve, Adriana and Lily would stay up all night together in Lily's home. In fact, looking back on her childhood, most of the celebrations she fondly remembers took place in Lili's house. That last night they shared together in the hotel room in Bucharest, Lily was sad and even cried a little at the thought of Adriana moving so far away, and knew that in just a few short hours Adriana would be gone and her life would never be the same again.

In so many ways Lily was different from Adriana. Even though Romania had its issues, Lily never wanted to leave her home. As an adult, after the factory she worked at as an electrical mechanic closed its doors in the wake of the revolution, Lily did work once and a while in other European countries as a housekeeper to earn extra foreign dollars, but she always returned home. On the other hand, Adriana wanted to leave her home and was not remorseful, and in fact was very excited about the new life that was waiting for her in Canada.

The next morning they got up early and made their way to the heavily guarded Bucharest International Airport. Under communism the military was everywhere in Romania, and especially at the airports. Military personnel holding machine guns guarded the doors, searched passengers entering and leaving security, and even stood under little shelters guarding the runways. As planes landed and took off, you could look out the window and see a row of tiny narrow shelters that lined the runways. Each shelter housed an armed solider.

Before crossing the line that separated escorts from the passengers, Adriana and her mother hugged and kissed her family good-bye that morning, in a combination of sad tears and excitement, as they left their family and life in Romania to begin their new life half a world away. Lily stood in the background with tears in her eyes as she watched armed guards search Adriana before she turned to wave good-bye and disappear down a long corridor that led to the passenger waiting area.

They flew that morning from Bucharest to Frankfurt, Germany

by Tarom, the national airline of Romania. On that flight, Adriana sat in a window seat beside a German man and only knew a few worlds of English at the time. With a heavy ascent, she could awkwardly say "Coke," and "Cloud." Sitting beside the young German man on that flight she recalled to me years later that looking out the window of the aircraft en-route to Frankfurt she pointing to a fluffy white formation in the sky, looked over at the young man sitting beside her, nodded at him and said, "Cloud." She felt good about being able to use an English word in the context of the real world. It is hard to believe that ten years later when Adriana and I returned to Romania she could speak English so well that her former grade school English teacher, whom we met while walking through her home town one morning, was too embarrassed to speak to her in English, and opted to only communicate with her in Romanian. From Frankfurt they flew to New York, where they met some Romanian people who were expecting them. Adriana does not remember much about who they were, but knows that someone made arrangements for these people to help her and her mother navigate their way through the airport. They were in the New York airport only a few hours before catching a fight to Toronto.

They left Bucharest early in the morning and arrived in Toronto around 10 pm that night. With the time change, they were in transit almost twenty-four hours that day. Even with the long day, Adriana was too excited to be tired. As the aircraft circled Pearson International Airport in preparation for landing, she looked out the window and was so impressed with all of the lights of Toronto illuminating the nighttime landscape in a mass of yellow and white star-like clusters that seemed to merge together and dissipate as far as the eye could see in gridline formation. Once the aircraft came to a standstill on the runway, with their life in Romania and all of their possessions gone forever, they emerged from the aircraft and followed a long corridor leading to the Canadian customs.

As they were presenting their papers and checking through their luggage, Adriana's excitement grew as she turned and caught sight of her sister waving at her through the glass wall that separated customs from the rest of the airport. Once on the other side, there was a tearful reunion, as they hugged and kissed each other before making their way out of the airport to embark on the ninety-minute drive from Toronto to Orangeville. Mariana had told Adriana that she lived only fifteen minutes out of town, and Adriana thought she meant fifteen minutes out of Toronto. On the trip home that night, she kept wondering just where she was going, as it seemed to be taking forever to get to her sister's home. It was almost 1 a.m. when they finally arrived in Orangeville. Adriana stepped out of the car and walked across that very driveway where she and I were destined to meet in three years' time, and looked in the darkness of the night at the silhouette of the low profile bungalow that was now her new home. She stayed up until almost 4 a.m. since her sister had a big feast planned in celebration of her arrival.

The next day she traveled into Orangeville with her sister, where she walked through the mall and found herself totally amazed by the number of stores and the incredibly large selection of merchandise available to the consumer. She was particularly impressed with K-Mart at the far end of the mall. Accustomed to Romania where there were so many shortages, it was almost overwhelming to look at the multitude of stores and selection of merchandise. While it was overwhelming to see so much in the stores, it was also a little hard, since she had no money and could not purchase any of the items she was looking at.

Shortly after arriving in Canada, she enrolled in the grade ten program at the Orangeville High School and was placed in an English as a second language classroom. She worked hard to learn to speak and write in English. As well, her niece and nephew helped her to learn the language, and she learned a lot by watching cartoons with the two children. She had very few friends, since Orangeville was a rather cliquey place. Her only real friends were the other students in the English as a second language class, until a few years later when she met my cousin Caroline in a grade twelve cooking class. Caroline became her only real friend. While the other girls did not make friends with her, she was very pretty, and the boys did make a fuss over her. She worked hard and completed high school by the end of term one in 1986, and worked for half a year before starting the nursing program in Toronto. I always admired the brave and adventurous spirit within her heart. She left everything behind; learned a new language, and started over in a foreign county.

During the fall of 1988 the part of the world that Adriana emerged from was about to be changed forever with the systematic collapse of every communist regime in Eastern Europe – starting with Poland in September, followed by Hungary in October and the dismantling of the Berlin Wall in November. From the fall of 1988 until 1992 we watched the collapse of communism in Easter Europe, including the once mighty Soviet Union, and observed a realignment of world powers that emerged from the dust and debris of the Iron Curtain that laid in ruins. During the fall of 1989, Adriana and I did talk a little about the emerging political changes taking hold in Eastern Europe, and she always seemed to feel that the political reforms that were under way would not impact on Romania, since Ceausescu's grip on the nation was too tight. She whole-heartedly believed that he would never allow reform to shake the foundations of the communist regime that elevated him so far above the rest of humanity.

I was amazed at the news broadcasts showing the political tension and the final demise of the communist regime in Romania between December 15 and Christmas Day. Adriana and I talked on the phone just about every day from the time I arrived in Elliot Lake until the day before her arrival. Even though her family in Romania was far from the conflict and chaos that we were watching on television, during our conversations that week I could hear and sense the concern in her voice for her family back home, as the growing political tension and turmoil seemed to be escalating daily. Even though the chaos was gaining momentum, Adriana was still convinced that Ceausescu's grip on the country was just too tight to shake him from power. However, the country was falling apart fast, with an outpouring of mass hysteria that was sweeping across her homeland.

I remember watching on television Ceausescu and his wife standing side by side on the balcony overlooking the enraged masses that were gathering before him, as he pleaded for people to not forfeit the gains they have made under the current socialist system. He had just returned from a state visit to Iran to find his country in chaos. The revolution began in the city of Timisoara on December 15, 1989 as thousands of Romanians entered into combat with the Securitate, Nicoloe Ceausescu's special police force. As tension grew in Romania that week, a state of emergency was declared and Ceausescu's personal bodyguard actually killed the minister of defense when he refused to order the military to open fire on the demonstrators. Following this, the military did combat the demonstrators for a short while before they changed sides and joined the demonstrators and began to battle against the Securitate who remained loyal to Ceausescu and his regime. With tension peaking, there was word in the western media of heavy fighting in Bucharest, Sibu and Timisoara. As the week progressed, clashes between the demonstrators, backed by the military against the Securitate, moved in a little closer to Adriana's family as fighting took hold in Arad, Brasov and Cluj. While her hometown of Tirnaveni was spared, the armed conflict and turmoil that was highlighted in the western media, violence and armed conflicts were taking root to the north, south and east of her hometown. As the nation's political structures collapsed under mass political pressure, anarchy and chaos spread across the country in small pockets of upheaval. The country was falling apart fast, and it was difficult to say at the time just how far and wide spread the turmoil and fighting would extend before either the regime actually collapsed or reestablished its control. I remember news flashes showing armored vehicles moving around Bucharest, and hearing that Ceausescu and his family had fled by helicopter, only to learn on Christmas morning that he and his wife were captured, condemned in a secret trial, and executed before a firing squad on Christmas morning. I can still see the pictures that aired on television that morning of Ceausescu and his wife's lifeless and aged bodies as they slouched over each other against a concrete wall. Romania's Christmas present to itself that year were the lead-pierced aged and lifeless bodies of Nicoloe and Elena Ceausescu.

Romania was emerging from behind the Iron Curtain to take its place in the world.

In the wake of the executions, Romania expressed a mass hysteria and demonstration of free will. One news flash showed an immense rally outside of Ceausescu's palace in the capital city, with people shouting and chanting. In the middle of this, one man was reading poetry he wrote. He held his papers in his hand and shouted so that the world would finally hear his words that had been banned for so long. The demonstrations formulated into an unbridled hysteria, as Romania celebrated its newfound freedoms.

Ceausescu was a ruthless dictator and his family did extend privileges to themselves at the expense and suffering of the general masses. Of all the revolutions that spread across Eastern Europe that fall the one in Romania was the most violent and unruly. Having said that, one debt of gratitude I do owe the man is the legislation he enacted to outlaw contraceptives and abortions in the late 1960's. Adriana once told me that it was in fact those laws that allowed her to come into the world, since in those days abortions performed at home were one of the few effective methods of birth control available to the general population.

As Adriana and I talked on the phone Christmas afternoon shortly after western news broadcast the secret trial and execution of Nicole and Elena Ceausescu I could hear the celebration in her home and the excitement in her voice at hearing that after almost forty year of oppression, Romania was now a free nation. I didn't intend to dampen the celebrations, but I did suggest that perhaps a sudden shift to a capitalist based economy would not necessarily fill empty cupboards. As Adriana's homeland stood on the threshold of a new future, it was exciting to have a connection with this revolution and the long and painful road that lay ahead of Romania as it began the process of merging into the western world after existing for years in isolation behind closed doors. The world had moved on since Romania fell behind the Iron Curtain in the post war years, and it would take considerable time and growing pains for it to catch-up and merge into the western economic and political culture. Nevertheless, as with all new endeavors, there was a certain excitement that Christmas morning as Adriana's homeland emerged from isolation to take its new place in the world. With global politics quickly shifted to the back burner, we looked with anticipation to finally being together in Elliot Lake the following day.

Chapter 32

Boxing Day

It is hard to believe that only a year previous I was only hoping for the opportunity to meet Adriana again, and now, twelve months later, she and I were engaged and she was about to spend part of the Christmas holiday with my family and me – and in another 12 months we would actually be newlyweds of five months. I was anxious all day as I anticipated her arrival. As the hours passed I kept track of where she was en-route to Elliot Lake, and my excitement grew with each passing half hour. The day seemed to drag on forever, until she and Len finally arrived late in the evening. I borrowed Dad's car and was at the bus stop an hour before her arrival, restlessly waiting for her. My heart lifted when I saw her step down from the bus, and we moved towards each other for a short embrace and a passionate kiss, as our lips and bodies seemed to momentarily mold together for a brief few seconds, while Len stood just behind Adriana. In those days Adriana and I were always touching and kissing each other. Just about anywhere and anytime we would hold hands, kiss or hug each other, and it did not really matter where we were or who was around. As the years passed we still will embrace in a short quick hug, a peck on the lips and move along holding hands. We are still as much in love twenty years later as we were then.

One evening Len, Adriana and I made our way to the Royal Canadian Legion with my friend Nelson, who had returned on leave from the Canadian Air Force, where he served as a radio technician. After spending an evening there, the four of us stopped at the lower plaza sub shop for a combo before walking home. This was the usual routine for Nelson and me, following an evening at the Legion. That particular night I remember being a little embarrassed with myself as we made our way to the sub shop. As the four of us were walking across the upper plaza parking lot nearing the steps by Canada Post, Nelson and I became absorbed in some deep conversation and I did not notice that Adriana had actually fallen a little behind. Len noticed Adriana walking alone about ten feet in the rear and made a point of stopping and walking with her. When I realized what I had done, I stopped and waited with an apology for her to catch-up to me before moving on with Nelson. After leaving the sub shop the four of us embarked on the long cold walk home, as we made our way to Ontario Street and continued on up Hillside North. It was a three kilometer walk in the cold of winter, as Mom and Dad in those days still lived at 57 Dieppe Avenue. It was during this walk that I made up for my inconsideration of walking too far ahead of Adriana earlier in the evening by giving her my underwear. It was a cold crisp night with temperatures dropping down to -25C, and this temperature was in slight contrast to Adriana, who was wearing her sexy black leather miniskirt and black nylons. She never did dress warmly enough for the weather, and it seems that for as long as I can remember I am always taking off my clothes to provide her with protection from the elements. In fact one time in the summer of 1992 Adriana and I traveled halfway around the world together, and she refused to bring a jacket for the journey because the afternoon that we embarked on our expedition was particularly sunny and warm. As a result of that decision, I spend a few cool evening in the

Romanian countryside next to Adriana, snuggled nice and warm in my jacket. About half way home that cold December evening in 1989 she froze her legs, and by the time we reached the Hillside Plaza she was almost in tears. With few options, I used my bankcard to open the 24-hour Northern Credit ATM access door and went inside to remove my long underwear while Adriana stood watch. She then went into the bank machine room and slipped her long slender sexy legs into my long-johns, as I stood watch. From the Northern Credit instant bank machine/clothing exchange center we walked to the far end of the plaza and sat on the sidewalk in front of the Mr. Doughnut coffee shop. Nelson, Len, Adriana and I intended on sitting down together for one last cup of coffee before retiring for the night. Unfortunately the restaurant had closed early, so the four of us just sat on the sidewalk outside and talked for about twenty minutes before the police arrived to express concerns about a certain small group of people loitering on the streets of Elliot Lake in the early hours of the morning. In my typical condescending manner I stood up and walked towards the police officers as they disembarked from their vehicle. Before they had a chance to say much I said, "Hey man, we are all out of luck here, this doughnut shop is closed, you're going to have to move along and find another one." In an odd sort of way they did not quite get the humour in my comment and directed us on down the road to an all-night corner store in the Paris Plaza. With Adriana now in the warmth of my long underwear, the four of us made our way to the Paris Plaza for a cup of coffee before parting ways with Nelson and continuing on our 3 km walk home. It was one of those nights that you just did not want to end.

The following day Len took a Gray Coach back to Toronto. Adriana and I remained in town until January 1, before making our journey south. Sometime between the night at the Legion and New Years Eve, Adriana and I made our way back to the Algo Inn for an evening alone. As usual, I would wait outside while Adriana booked into the room as a lonely out-of-town visitor using her Toronto address, so that people would not suspect that we were just two kids taking a room for the evening. We then followed our traditional route hand in hand, up the sidewalk to the roof ramp that led us to the upper parking lot and across the roof to the upper hotel entrance where we could gain access to our room without having to walk past the main desk. It was this feature that made the Algo Inn one of our most favourite locations for an evening alone.

New Years Eve was our final night in Elliot Lake, before heading south to begin the winter semester. It was at this point I learned about the Romanian tradition of staying up all night and not eating chicken on New Years Eve, because eating chicken would cause one to go backwards in the coming year. Adriana was always fond of her Romanian holiday traditions that included homemade Turkish Delight sweetbread, pork jelly, Russian salad, mititei and cabbage rolls, all enhanced by a nice selection of wines and hard alcohol. As a child in Romania, the Christmas tree in her house was decorated with candles that were never actually lit, along with apples and nuts. As well, even to this day, she fondly remembers singing Christmas carols door to door with a small group of children, and collecting money at each household they visited. She would often earn as much as one hundred lei during an evening of caroling, which was a fair wage for a child, since an afternoon at the movies only cost ten lei. One time when Adriana was a young girl a number of boys her age arrived at the door singing carols while she was home alone. She invited the boys in and gave them all a glass of wine and some sweetbread that her mother had made for the holidays. The boys did not take off their shoes and had muddied up the kitchen. As Adriana was enjoying her evening, someone shouted, "YOUR MOTHER IS COMING HOME!" Catching a glimpse of her mother walking down the road, in a panic she unsuccessfully tried to get everyone out of the house. When her mother found all of the boys and the mess in the kitchen, she sent Adriana to her room and told her to wait until her father came home. Adriana went to bed that night praying that her mother would not report to Mr. Sas the events of the evening, and to Adriana's great relief the next day, her father did not appear to be any the wiser. Parents often pick their battles, and I always suspected that her mother did say something to Mr. Sas, and he most likely laughed a little and decided to let the incident slide.

On the other hand, in my family, the holidays consisted of a wonderful turkey meal on Christmas day. I always loved my mother's stuffing! New Year's Eve consisted of my family getting together and ordering Chinese takeout, and for this particular year it was without chicken balls and chicken wings in order to avoid going backwards in the coming year. As well that year, Kim made a large bowl of rum-eggnog, and following Kim's recipe, Adriana and I still make it for the holidays. I can still see Adriana drinking eggnog and dancing in the upper living room in the early hours of the morning. She looked incredible! We stayed up all night even though the following day we had to travel back to Toronto and Waterloo.

With only one broken teacup to her credit this holiday season, on January 1st we caught a bus to Sudbury, where we boarded a Toronto-bound train. Due to the high volume of holiday travelers there were no economy tickets available, so we had to settle for a more expensive roomette in first class. Once on the train we were directed to a cramped little room with two seats that were not entirely comfortable, and they were situated across from a toilet bowl. I remember thinking at the time that this will not be the most comfortable trip, and the toilet bowl across from our seat just seemed to spoil the mood. However, as fate would have it, the mood lifted considerably when the gentleman in the next room told us that the bench actually folds out into a double bed. The train hardly got moving before we had the door closed, the bed pulled and our clothing off. I remember thinking at the time that if the train ever went off the tracks we would be in a fine mess, with the two of us covered with nothing but a single white bed sheet. Not being properly prepared for this trip, this trip led into another one of those occasions when we had to wait a month before knowing for sure that the two of us were not becoming three in a nine short months. In many ways this was sort of an historic trip, since the train we boarded in Sudbury was the last transcontinental run for Via Rail. As the train slowly chugged and wound its way across the southern reaches of the Canadian Shield and into the fertile snow-covered farmland of Southern Ontario it weaned out an era of transcontinental transit that dated back over a century. The train was actually delayed for several hours near Parry Sound. Somewhat curious about the long delay and noting that my 11:30 p.m. Grey Coach connection in Toronto was looking less likely as the hours slipped by, I peeked around the curtain and looked through the frost-covered window. I could see nothing but the cold winter darkness that surrounded the warmth of our encampment. As the train pulled into Union Station I remember the two of us scrambling to get dressed again before the train came to a stop. The train left around four in the afternoon, and we arrived in Toronto around 12 a.m., which left me stranded in Toronto. By the time the train came to a stop, we and had the bed pushed up behind the bench seat in time to disembark. Just as we were about to leave the roomette a conductor came by and asked if we had used the bed, and after listening to our response, he seemed a little upset as he said, "I will have to change the sheets now," and as we were walking out of the car I could hear him mumble under his breath as he pulled the bed out and removed the sheets. Listening to him, I thought to myself, "Give us a break. It's the last run of the transcontinental and we wanted to make it a memorable trip!"

At any rate, I had more concerns on my mind at the time, as I almost simultaneously wondered to myself if Adriana was pregnant and how was I going to get to Waterloo. Adriana and I walked hand in hand into Union Station carrying nothing but a small backpack. We traveled so light in those days. As we moved along, I overheard a conversation between two other passengers who missed their connections. According to their conversation, Via Rail was going to transport by taxi all travelers with a transfer ticket to their final destination. I told Adriana that I will just blend in with the other travelers that had a Via Rail transfer ticket and get a free taxi ride to Waterloo, so we kissed good night and she caught a subway home, as I scammed a free taxi ride back to Waterloo complements of Via Rail.

When I arrived home that evening, I found John and Jay sitting in the upper living room having a few drinks and sharing their holiday adventures, so I opened a bottle of cheap Scotch and joined them.

Chapter 32

Our Usual Weekend Date

As usual, Adriana and I talked on the phone a lot that week and met again in Waterloo on the following weekend. She spent just about every weekend with me in Waterloo that year. We maintained our routines: on Friday evening I sat on the third floor of the Arts Library studying as I waited for her to arrive. I always sat by the window hoping that I could catch a glimpse of her as she crossed the campus and made her way into the library, but I never did see her, and was always pleasantly surprised when I looked up from my books to see her walking towards me. My heart lifted with joy as I looked up and saw her moving towards my table. I stood up as we met and embraced in a kiss. She had a small backpack that she carried over her shoulder with her books and her clothing for the weekend. We never studied much on a Friday evening. Instead we always went out on a date, usually to a movie followed by a meal at one of our favourite restaurants at the University Plaza, or we would spend the evening at one of the campus pubs, either Federation Hall or the Bombshelter, and would usually end the evening at the Campus Center sharing a cup of coffee and dropping a few quarters into the Black Knight before walking back to my basement apartment on 56 Helene Crescent.

That particular evening we went to the Sub shop and shared a twelve inch seafood sub. It was our favouite sub. As we stood in line I asked Adriana if she wanted to share a seafood sub as usual, and she responded by simply looking at me and responding, "I am." I looked at her somewhat concerned and responded, "You are!" and she nodded and said, "Yes, I am." I then glanced over at the server and said, "One seafood on white with olives and hot peppers," as I made the quick calculation that she will only be seven months by the time of our wedding. After paying for the sub we found a table for two near the window. I sat across from her thinking to myself that our life was about to get a little more complicated. As I was about to take a bite from my sub, Adriana looked at me and said, "I just wanted to see what you would say." I simply looked over at her and said, "You're not!" to which she simply replied, "I'm not." Adriana still did not really think I was for real, and this was her little way of testing me. I suspect that the simple fact that I did not go running out the door screaming with my hands frantically waving in a panic never to be seen again was a flying pass for me on this little test.

After eating we made our way to Federation Hall where we had a few beers and danced. I always loved the way she looked and felt when we were dancing. Adriana loved to dance, and I never really took her out dancing enough. If there is one thing I could go back and change, it would be to take her out dancing more. When she danced she always had a certain aura about her. For quicker dances she would sway her body to the music, and her head would slowly move from side to side, and she would look into my eyes and smile. For the slower dances she would move in close to me, almost as if our bodies were gently merging together, with her arms around my upper body and her head resting on my shoulder as we slowly moved back and forth to the music. Sometimes she would put her arms around my neck, and move her upper body out a little from me, as she tilted her head a little to the left, looking into my eyes and smiling as her body slowly swayed with mine to the music. Even to this day when we dance together it still feels the same.

Holding each other close, we danced for the rest of the evening before walking home for the night. She was wearing her pink jacket that night and I was wearing my leather University of Waterloo jacket that I wore year round. Leaving Fed. Hall, we walked arm and arm down the university circle lane to the Campus Center, where we sat close to each other in a secluded dark corner of the Great Hall sharing a cup of coffee and talking about things that have long since slipped into forgotten memories. Before stepping out into the cold damp night air, we went into the arcade for a few runs at the Black Knight. Then we continued on down the circle lane that led to a short trail that took us to the corner of University Avenue and Westmount Drive.

As we walked down the dimly lit trail that cool winter evening, holding Adriana by the hand, I told her about the Anglican Church and what my family endured. I did not tell her everything that evening; we seldom ever mentioned the subject again, and it was perhaps twenty years before I eventually told her everything, but that evening over twenty years ago, I told her enough. As I talked, she moved her head to my shoulder as we slowly moved along the path together. I could hear some sniffling, and as we passed under a dim trail light, I caught in the corner of my eye tears silently rolling down her cheeks.

In silence, with her body pulled in close to mine, we walked up University Avenue to Keats Way, turned left on Karen Walk and right on Helene Crescent. It was about 12:30 a.m. when we arrived home, and John McDonald was still up watching a late night talk show. He spent most of his university days in front of a twelve-inch colour television. As usual we made a few minutes of small talk with John before retiring for the night.

At this time Adriana was a second year nursing student. Once a semester she and her classmates would get together for a party, where they would bring a gag-gift wrapped with no name attached. The gifts were placed in a general pot and each girl would have to take a present and unwrap it in front of everyone. The intent was to contribute items that were embarrassing and usually sexually orientated. They would each select and unwrap a package and everyone would have a good laugh. Adriana would end up with some odd little novelties from these parties. Looking through her backpack that evening in my bedroom, she said, "Look what I got!" as she pulled out from this semester's particular party a pair of handcuffs.

Following our usual tried and tested hit-or-miss birth control practices we fell asleep holding each other on my narrow futon bed. And this night, like so many others, was followed by yet another month of wondering if we "are" or "are not." We were young and reckless, taking chances without really thinking of long-term consequences. In the next room, on the other side of our paper-thin wall was John McDonald. I never really thought about it at the time, but looking back we were not very concerned about what anyone heard or thought of what we were doing. John was an easily agitated person, and we must have driven him nuts.

The following morning as usual, we got up before John to have a shower together. We were both very thin at the time, and could easily fit in the four square foot shower cubical together as we embraced, washed and kissed each other. I can still see Adriana, with the water beading and running down her face, her long wet black hair slicked back over her shoulders, dripping water down her back as I would put my hands on either side of her face to tell her that I loved her, before we embraced in a long and passionate kiss under the warm water. After breakfast we always walked to the university library hand in hand. There we would settle in for a quiet day of studying, either sitting at a table across from each other on the third floor, or up a few levels at two study cubicles side by side. For so many years I so often sat all alone in the library diligently studying, and after so many years of solitude, even though we did not talk very much during these study sessions, it was comforting to have Adriana sitting next to me. Of course we would occasionally kiss, but for the most part it was serious work.

We always diligently studied until noon, then went for a lunch break at one of the restaurants next door in University Plaza or the Bomshelter. Afterwards, we returned to the library to study until early in the evening. Usually around mid afternoon we would pack up our books for a one-hour break, as we walked hand in hand over to the Campus Center for a cup of coffee and a few games of pinball before going back to the library until seven or eight o'clock in the evening. After a day of studying in the Arts Library, we would often walk hand in hand, each with a study backpack over one shoulder, as we made our way towards the Bombshelter or would catch a city bus to a movie and dinner. We were students and it just seemed so natural to carry our book bags as we went out for the evening, instead of making the long walk back to my apartment to drop them off. Late in the evening, or in the early hours of the morning, we found our way back to my little basement apartment for an evening to rival the previous night's events. The only difference between Saturday night and Friday night was that Adriana's chin was a little reddish, and we knew that the following morning we would be parting ways, since Adriana would head back to Toronto for another week. We always held each other a little closer on Saturday nights.

That particular Saturday, after a long day dedicated to studying, I remember we watched a movie called Sex Lies and Video Tapes at the Waterloo Theater on King Street. On the way back to the university that cool damp winter evening under a light snowfall we stopped at the Mongolian's Grill, a rather fancy, expensive restaurant at the back corner of University Plaza, just by the dirt trail at the rear of the plaza that led to the university. We had passed the restaurant many times, but always felt that it was a little too expensive for our budget. That evening it felt so nice holding hands as we stepped into the warmth of the building, where a gentleman greeted us, took our jackets and led us to a quiet little table for two off to the side. Sitting across from each other in the lushness of our surroundings perusing the menu, we realized that this fine establishment was a little out of our price range. We ordered a cup of green tea each and shared the most beautiful chocolate sunday I ever had the pleasure of tasting. Even though we never did return to the Mongolian's Grill, that evening remains a beautiful memory for Adriana and me. Before making our way home we stopped at the Bomshelter for a beer and played a few pinball games.

Sunday mornings were always the same as Saturday mornings, starting with a shower, followed by breakfast and then studying at the library. The only difference was that Adriana would catch a city bus sometime around 4 p.m. to the Kitchener Grey Coach station where she would transfer to a Toronto-bound Gray Coach. We usually parted ways for the week at the University bus stop near University Avenue across from the campus alumni shop and bookstore. It was always such a lonely feeling, as we stood there holding hands and kissing, knowing that in a few minutes we would be parting ways for another week. During these times we would look so forward to our wedding day, knowing that we would no longer have to part again each weekend. Sometimes, Adriana and I would decide at the last minute to stay together for another night, and she would catch an early morning bus back to Toronto, but that particular weekend she returned to Toronto Sunday evening. When the bus arrived, Adriana sat at a window seat and blew me a kiss and waved good-bye. Standing at the bus stop alone with my daypack over my left shoulder watching the bus merge into traffic and disappear down University Avenue I had such a lonely and empty feeling in me. I just felt so sad.

Chapter 34

The Weary Rose

My winter break finally arrived in mid February of that year, and I made arrangements to meet with Adriana in Toronto on Friday evening, en route to Elliot Lake. She was unable to travel home with me that year, since her college did not have a spring break at the same time as the University of Waterloo. Since Valentine's Day was only four days away, and I would be in Elliot Lake at that time, I bought Adriana a card and a single red rose before I made my way to the Kitchener Grey Coach terminal to catch a late afternoon coach to Toronto. That would provide me with at least six hours with Adriana before I had to catch the red-eye north. I arrived in the city around 6 p.m. that evening and found Adriana waiting for me in the terminal.

As we embraced and kissed, I gave her my rose for Valentine's Day. It was mid winter and the uncovered rose was already starting to wilt a little by the time I presented it to her, and as the evening wore on, it began to look more and more flailed around the edges. From the bus terminal we walked hand in hand that cool February evening down the street and made our way to the Eaton's Center, where we sat outside on a bench under a streetlight and exchanged cards. As we read each other's Valentine's card, Adriana's face filled with tears. Taking me by both hands, she looked into my eyes and asked me one last time if I was sure that I wanted to marry her. I moved my hand upward, and gently caressed either side of her face, as I looked into the warmth of her big brown tear-filled eyes, and told her how much I loved her, and that I could not even begin to imagine my life without her. On the verge of tears myself, we kissed as I wiped the tears from her cheeks with my fingers. Pulling back a little from me, and placing her hands over my hands that still rested on either side of her face, said to me, "Then we will never talk about this again." Standing up, she put her left arm around the back of my mid-body and pulled herself into me with her other hand still holding her ever-wilting rose, as we walked into the Eaton's Center. By this time the head of the rose actually began to droop a little, and the petal ends were starting to curl. As we moved forward together, our paths continued to merge, and we knew in our hearts that each step we took brought us one step closer to the final merging of our two paths. As we walked into the Eaton's Center, I remember looking up and seeing this incredible display of Canada Geese flying in "V" formation just below a high ceiling skylight. We did a lot of window shopping that evening and finally started to make our way back to the bus terminal around 10 p.m., so that I could catch my 11:30 p.m. bus north.

On our way back to the bus terminal, we became a little confused with direction and eventually asked an elderly street person for instructions how to get back to the bus station. Instead of giving us directions he offered to guide us. I cautiously accepted his offer, since he was a perfect stranger to me, and I did not really trust him; however, he was elderly and about half my size, so I decided that should he attempt to misguide Adriana and me, he could pose no more than a minimal threat. He proved to be honest enough, and guided us back to the bus station, and as it turned out, we were only a few blocks from the station when we stopped to ask him for help.

Since we still had a little time left, the gentleman accepted our offer to buy him a coffee at the dingy little café across the street. Once there, he took a seat beside me, while Adriana laid the drooping rose on the table and took a seat directly across. In fact the rose was starting to look quite dreadful. The head was completely drooped over with its curled, wilted and frail edges starting to turn a little blackish. No sooner did we sit at a table than a waitress walked over, looked at the gentleman that accompanied us and sternly said, "I told you to never come back here again!" I looked up and replied, "He's with us," and ordered three cups of coffee that arrived in less than a minute. It was a little diner with orange plastic seats attached to dirty grey tables with a disgusting white tile floor covered with small pools of dirty water and cigarette butts. A long coffee bar with a string of plastic-covered orange bar stools lined the side of the restaurant overlooking a greasy kitchen. It was your typical greasy spoon, and they seemed to know the gentleman well at this fine establishment and were anxious for him to leave.

We sat in the restaurant sipping coffee and talking to the gentleman about his life on the streets. Adriana asked him why he took the option of sleeping outside when there are warm hostels in the downtown core, and he explained that he did not like the rules of the hostels and preferred the freedom of the streets. Apparently the hostels made the guests take a shower! He earned his money from handouts and often ate at a church soup kitchen somewhere in the downtown core. He wore a long black wool overcoat, and as he shifted his weight on the chair, his jacket opened a little, revealing his street survival gear. Inside his jacket he had a small club that I assumed was for protection, a long metal flashlight and a cutlery set all held in place with silver duct tape and thread. He had everything in his jacket that he needed for life on the streets of Toronto. Adriana was so good about talking to him and asking him all kinds of questions about his life on the street and where he came from. Working and talking with elders was a gift that she had that worked well for her years later, when she found her calling working with the elderly – first as a home care nurse and then as a nurse on an extended care unit. Sitting in the dingy little café in the core of Toronto talking to that elderly gentleman so many years ago, I could see the love and passion that she had for the elderly. While talking to him that evening, he never did tell us his name, but we did learn that he was a fellow northerner who was raised by his uncle Gerrard LaPlante in Timmins.

After about twenty minutes we left the little diner. We tried to part ways with the elderly gentleman some time around 11 p.m.; however, he followed us to the bus station where I gave him a five-dollar bill, and thanked him for his company. Alone again with Adriana and her wilting rose now completely drooped over and trimmed in a blackish touch of frostbite, I walked her back to the Subway station before catching my bus north. She wanted to remain at the bus station to see me off, but I was afraid to have her walk alone to the subway so late in the evening, and convinced her to let me walk her to the subway station; otherwise, I would have worried all the way home. Arm in arm, with our bodies leaning into each other, we left the bus terminal and walked up Bay Street until we hit Gerrard and then walked over to Young Street, where I left Adriana at a subway stop. We stood at the top of the stairs leading to the underground transit kissing and holding each other, wishing the minutes would start passing like hours rather than seconds. With time running short, we slowly pulled away from each other as I watched Adriana with her reddish-black, drooping, wilted rose in hand walk down the stairs and disappear around the corner. It seemed we were always parting ways.

On the way to the subway with Adriana, I was very conscious of the direction I was walking, so that I could find my way back to the bus terminal. However, on my return trip I became a little lost and found myself standing at the very corner where Adriana and I met that elderly street person only an hour ago. Catching my baring, I looked up and laughed to myself as I realized that we met him on the corner of Gerrard and Laplante. With Adriana on my mind, I made my way back to the bus terminal, and boarded the coach for the long ride north, while all the time looking forward to the following weekend when I could take Adriana in my arms and kiss her again. As I took my seat in the bus, feeling so very lonely for Adriana, I could only think of our upcoming wedding, with the knowledge that in six months I would finally be with the woman whom I so deeply loved. I had never been in love before, and had never felt this way about anyone. Adriana was, and still is, so special to me.

When I arrived home the following morning, Dad was waiting for me at the Elliot Lake bus stop. He always came alone to pick me up, never allowing anyone else to accompany him. Meeting me at the bus stop was his special thing that he always did. As I stepped off the bus, I saw him standing on the sidewalk waiting for me with his silvery gray hair, wearing his gray parka and blue jeans. I always looked forward to seeing him when I arrived home from university, and I know that he was always proud to be picking me up, knowing that I was returning home from my studies down south. When I would step down from the bus I never hugged him, but rather optioned for a good solid handshake. Looking back, I wish I had just put my arms around him, hugged him and told him how much I loved him. I know he loved me. Afterwards, he always drove me home to Mom, who was anxiously waiting at home for my arrival. She always met me at the door with a hug and a kiss. When I arrived home that year they had a few packages of crabmeat in the fridge. Having never eaten it before, I remember finding it so tasty, covered in butter and nuked in the microwave for a half a minute.

The week past quickly. It consisted of several late evenings drinking coffee with Dad at Peachy's Restaurant. Whenever I was home, Dad and I would usually walk up the road to this restaurant and spend the evening talking as we drank several cups of coffee. Our conversations generally focused on mining as we discussed options for his mineral claims near Matheson, Ontario, as well as conversations regarding the federal government's lack of proper support for our armed forces, and current religious trends in contemporary society. Politics, religion and mining pretty much summed up the content of our conversations over the years. I am grateful for those conversations with Dad, since it allowed me to really get to know him – what he thought, and how he felt about things. In many ways those conversations were as much a part of my education as any university course I ever completed. In so many ways Dad was my pilot. I relied on his guidance and advice to shape my perspective on the world around me, and after his death, my understanding and knowledge of his view on certain topics and his perception of the world became my most valuable sounding board. As the years passed, whenever I found myself trying to understand a moral dilemma or attempting to make sense of the world around me, I could always go back to those conversations with my Dad and reflect on what his take would be on a similar situation. In so many ways my Dad was my first teacher. Through him I learned the lessons in life I needed to make sense of the world around me and to find my place in a manner that was guided and governed by values. In a world where people so often seem lost living day to day, with so few guiding values to govern their decisions and actions, I felt secure in the lessons my father provided.

After spending a week with my family in Elliot Lake, I woke early the following Sunday morning and made my way south again, where I met my love. We decided that instead of spending just a few hours together in the city, she would accompany me to Waterloo, spend the night and return to Toronto the following morning in time to attend class. When we arrived back in Kitchener, we caught a city bus to the university, where we studied at the library until sometime around 9 p.m. As we were leaving the library, we met a friend named Prima-Donna Mitchell, who simply went by the name of Prima. She was a very outspoken native girl who had become friends with Adriana and me over the course of the year. Looking at Adriana and me, she asked if Adriana was in class the following day, since she knew that I had just returned from my spring break. Adriana said, "No, I just came so I could spend a little more time with Michael." Prima looked at us and quite bluntly said, "You two just want sex," before walking away.

Chapter 35

March Break

As the year continued to pass with the countdown to our wedding getting closer every day, Adriana and I continued to spend every weekend together. She always arrived early Friday evening and stayed until late Sunday evening or early Monday morning. We looked forward to each weekend with such anticipation and dreaded the arrival of Monday morning. The four or five nights we were apart each week seemed so long and monotonous while on the other hand, the weekends were so exciting and seemed to slip away all too quickly.

Looking back, some weekends stand out as memorable, or even an event or two seems to withstand the test of time, while other weekends seem to almost blend together and fade somewhat from memory with the passage of the years. One afternoon in mid March was one of those memories that seems to be elevated in a realm of its own and holds a special meaning and place in my heart. Due to the college strike earlier in the year, Adriana had a few days added to her school year just before Christmas and at the end of the year, in combination with a shorter spring break. This year her March break was actually in the month of March. With only a few days off, she made a visit to her sister and mother in mid-week, and then made arrangements to travel to Waterloo to see me. A bus connection between Orangeville and Waterloo did not exist, and it was even difficult to make a connection between Orangeville and Toronto, so Adriana managed to obtain a ride with my cousin John Underhill. He left Adriana at my apartment, where she found that no one was home. With a small daypack over her left shoulder she made her way from 56 Helene Crescent on route to the university, in hopes of finding me somewhere on campus. At the same time, I had just walked out of my last class for the afternoon and was making my way home. I remember that afternoon well. Spring came early to Waterloo that year. The snow had long since melted, and the dirty mucky days of spring had vanished sometime over the past few days. Walking home that afternoon under a warm, sunny, blue cloudless sky it was almost as if we were given a little tease of the summer to come. About half way home, looking down the sidewalk, I noticed Adriana walking towards me and for a split second, I was in disbelief. It was mid-week and I was not expecting her for another few days, so seeing her there that afternoon was one of those beautiful surprises in life when something wonderful and unexpected happens. Coming towards me in her black leather mini skirt, black nylons and a white-laced blouse, with her long gorgeous legs and her tall slender body she was so incredibly sexy! It was almost the same outfit that she wore that day seventeen months previous when I first met her. She looked absolutely breathtaking. We both had such big smiles on our faces as we came together that afternoon. As we met on the sidewalk, we hugged each other and kissed as I pulled back and told her how happy I was to see her. That unexpected spring encounter remains a beautiful and cherished gift that stands by itself as a memorable moment in life that I will treasure for the rest of my days. Adriana was just so beautiful and it was so unexpected meeting her there that afternoon. She told me that since she had the day off and John

Underhill was able to drive her into Waterloo, she decided to surprise me with a visit. She did not have to return to Toronto for class until Monday, so she had the rest of the week and the weekend with me in Waterloo. My time with Adriana from the first time we met and the years to follow is a timeless and cherished gift.

Instead of rushing on to the apartment, we headed back to the Campus Centre with our daypacks and spent the afternoon in the Bombshelter, where we met up with Prima, my cousin Sanford, and a few other friends. With the year coming to an end, we were both running a little low on cash, so we had no more that a beer each and enjoyed the good company of family and friends. Sanford and Prima got into a little argument, when Sanford discovered that she scored low on the LSAT, and would still gain entrance to a law degree program due to her First Nations' status, and Prima became a little upset with Sanford for suggesting that the political science program was a useless degree and further to the point, made reference to one of our department's outstanding professors as a "Birdbrain," knowing full well as he was making these outlandish comments that both Prima and I were fourth year political science students who had some admiration for the man he was so freely criticizing. In mid conversation, Sanford actually turned to me and said, "You agree that the man is a birdbrain, don't you?" My response was simple and to the point, as I clearly stated, "No, I don't agree!" It was a little embarrassing, and I apologized to Prima after he left. Prima said not to worry about it, because he was just bitter for not earning the grades he desired in the political science program and for not securing entry into a law degree program.

After spending an afternoon in the Bombselter, Adriana and I went back to my apartment, and I called my parents to ask for some money. Mom and Dad opened a bank account for me shortly after my birth where they deposited my first two baby bonus cheques to help pay for my education. But due to financial restraints, they were unable to maintain this contribution; thus, almost twenty-five years later, with accumulated interest, I had a total of one hundred and thirteen dollars and fifty-seven cents. I called Mom, and she made arrangements with my Aunt Vera to close my account and have the money transferred to my Royal Bank in Waterloo. The money arrived the following day, and I gave some of the money to Adriana so that she could purchase a one-way ticket to Toronto on Monday morning and a return ticket to visit me the following weekend. We used the rest of the money to enjoy our weekend together. I am sure that when Mom and Dad put that money away for me they were not thinking that I would be using it for a weekend with my girlfriend and to purchase her a bus ticket home. I do not know how we could afford it, but Adriana and I managed to see each other every weekend until I completed my studies that spring.

Chapter 36

Year End

With all but one final exam complete, I boarded a bus for home. I still had the last final to write for a correspondence history course that I took on industrialism in communist nations. That exam, I was allowed to write in my hometown high school. I didn't really think about it at the time, as I boarded the bus after finishing that fourth year in Waterloo, but it was my last trip home from school as a single young man. Nor did I reflect on how much my life had changed over those years and the changes that were about to come with my fast-approaching marriage to Adriana. Only four years previous Mom and Dad had driven me to Waterloo with Nancy in their big black Caprice Classic. I remember being so intimidated at the thought of living in a big city, attending university, and living on my own in a small bachelor apartment. Back in the fall of 1986, my graduation seemed so far away, and yet in retrospect, the time passed so fast.

As I boarded the bus for Toronto, I was looking forward to my short lay over in Toronto with Adriana. Due to the strike, she was still in school, with another two weeks of classes before completing the second year of her nursing program. She met me at the bus terminal, and we spent a little time together walking around the area hand in hand and talking. That afternoon we ate at a small pizza stand and made plans for when we would meet next. Adriana asked me if anyone would be meeting me at the "Turn Over." She meant to say, "Turn Off," in reference to the Highway 108 and 17 junction. English was still very much a second language to her, and I found the way she would misuse words once in a while so cute. We did not have much time together that afternoon, but even if only for a few hours, it was just so nice being with her.

After returning home, I started my last summer of employment working as a student for Parks and Recreation, where I tended to the town gardens of Elliot Lake. I usually finished my school year with a small amount of cash left over, with anywhere from a five hundred to two thousand dollars surplus, due to my frugal budgeting throughout the school year. However, after dating Adriana every weekend during the school year, I actually finished my fourth year completely broke and barely had enough money for my bus ticket home. With little money in hand, I sold my typewriter to Mom in exchange for funds to put my motorcycle on the road. Mom paid me $200 for the typewriter, which was about how much I spent on it the previous fall, and this was enough money for a few tanks of gas, a new set of spark plugs and an oil change.

Shortly after my arrival home, I made my way to the Elliot Lake Secondary High School, where I had spent five years previous to attending the University of Waterloo. I made my way to the library and wrote my final fourth year exam. This was the last degree requirement for my Bachelor of Arts program, and I was hoping that the grades would be submitted in time for my graduation in late May. As I sat in the ELSS library that morning waiting to write my final exam, Mr. Riddle, my high school vice principal told everyone to have their picture identification ready to present to him before they started writing. As he approached my table and handed me my exam, I attempted to show him my identification. He laughed, put the exam on the table in front of me and said, "I don't need to see I.D. from you Michael," before wishing me luck and moving on. I always admired Mr. Riddle. Standing almost six feet tall, he was a well-built man who dedicated countless hours to his students and the school. He supervised just about every school dance and spent hours before and after school teaching the driver education program. He taught almost every student in Elliot Lake to drive. Back in my high school days he would walk up to students and punch them in the arm, if they were not on task or doing something they should not be doing. When I was in grade ten, I handed him my school year book and asked him for his signature. He wrote, "Too Michael, my favourite punching bag!" Back in high school, receiving a good solid punch in the arm from Mr. Riddle was sort of a badge of honour. He made a real difference for his students, and looking back, there was no staff member who was more respected by the school's students. As the years passed I think of him once and a while, and the pain he went through when his daughter died in a tragic car accident a few years later on a return trip to the University of Western Ontario, following her winter break.

With my final exam out of the way and my marriage to Adriana fast approaching, I spent my days working for six dollars an hour, saving as much money as possible for my marriage. My evenings were consumed with writing resumes for job postings that I found in the Globe and Mail. I had actually started applying for just about any job that I was remotely qualified for, in the vain hope of securing employment in Toronto for the fall. The few responses that I received were very disappointing, with the exception of one from a gentleman working in municipal administration who noted that he had the same academic background as I did and wished me luck in finding a position somewhere.

As the weeks passed and I found myself in late May still looking for permanent work, I began to realize that I might be facing a winter on unemployment insurance, so long as I could work enough weeks during the summer months to qualify. This was not the promising start to my marriage and postgraduate life that I was hoping for and to add to my employment woes, Adriana and I had not even begun the process of securing residence in Toronto for the fall. Looking back we were so unprepared. Only three months before our marriage we were students with no income, no residence and no promising prospects of gainful employment.

Chapter 37

Graduation

With little money, Adriana and I had not seen each other for almost three weeks when we met in Waterloo for my Bachelor of Arts graduation on Thursday May 24, 1990. I arranged to take two days off work for my graduation, and that in turn provided me with four days to spend with Adriana. With our wedding date fast approaching, Mariana invited my family to spend the weekend with her, in order for the families to get to know each other a little and to make a contribution agreement arrangement between the families to cover the cost of the wedding.

Mom, Dad, Nancy and I left Elliot Lake early Wednesday afternoon. We drove to the South Bay Mouth ferry and down Highway 6 to Guelph, where we joined Highway 7 to Waterloo. While crossing on the ferry, we took a number of photos, and somehow, unknown to us at the time, we reused a film resulting in double takes. There was one picture of Mom and Nancy on the deck of the ferry, with a faded image of Adriana almost ghost-like standing beside them looking gorgeous in a blue formal dress, followed by a picture of me on the deck with the same ghost-like image of Adriana in the same blue dress, off to my side. Nancy wrote on the back of that picture, "This is a picture of Michael thinking about Adriana."

By the time we arrived in Waterloo, Dad and I were not getting along too well, and needed a little time apart. His health was poor, so I drove the car from Elliot Lake to Waterloo that day, and he was making for a very cantankerous backseat driver. He always loved getting behind the wheel, and I think he was having a difficult time accepting that his time operating a vehicle was coming to an end. Arriving in Kitchener, we went to the Grey Coach terminal and met Adriana, who had just arrived from Toronto. Following this, we drove to the Waterloo Inn, where we booked two rooms. I clearly remember Dad looking a little disturbed when Adriana and I booked into our own room.

Once in the privacy of our room, Adriana and I hugged and kissed. After three weeks apart, it was so good to hold her in my arms again. As usual, Adriana brought a bottle of red wine – to celebrate my graduation. We poured two glasses and sipped the wine as we sat in a rather small bathtub together, holding and kissing some more. After about a half hour of bathing and sipping wine, we received a call from the front desk asking us to please keep it down, out of respect for the other visitors in the establishment. Assuring the young lady that she must be calling the wrong room, I realized in a short while that I was actually talking to my sister Nancy who was staying with my parents just down the hall. Nancy wanted to do some shopping, so Adriana and I made arrangements to meet her in the lobby. We went shopping at the Conestoga Mall just across the road.

The next morning, Adriana and I slept in, and sometime around 10 a.m. I departed for the university to prepare for my graduation ceremony. Adriana and my family remained at the hotel and made arrangements to meet me outside of the Campus Center just prior to my graduation. Standing with my classmates outside of the Campus

Center in my black graduation gown, Adriana and my family found me, and Adriana presented me with one dozen red roses. I remember thinking at the time that no one ever gave me flowers for any reason before, but that was Adriana. She always had such a wonderful way of making someone feel so special by celebrating accomplishments. Standing beside me in the same blue dress from that ghost-like image in the ferry crossing picture with a dozen red roses in my hand, she put her arms around me, and snuggled right into me, as my sister Nancy snapped a picture of the two of us. She was so gorgeous and I always felt so proud to have her standing beside me. Following this, Adriana and my family took their seats amongst the thousands of onlookers, and I made my way through the graduation ceremony.

Following the ceremony, my family traveled to Orangeville, where we made a weekend visit with Adriana's family. There were a lot of people in the house that weekend: Adriana's mother, her sister's family, and Tibi and Daniel, her brother-in-law's nephew and wife who had just arrived from Romania. As we sat around the table that evening talking, Mariana and my mother agreed to pay $2000 each for the wedding. Unknown to Adriana's family, my parents had to take a bank loan for this.

The next day, I rented a U-hall trailer and drove my Dad's car back to Waterloo to collect my basement apartment furniture. I had made arrangements with my landlord to store my furniture there until my graduation. Since Tibi and Daniela were new to Canada, they accepted my invitation to accompany Adriana and me to Waterloo for the day, in order to see a little more of Canada. As we entered Waterloo, I was traveling a little slowly, since I was nervous moving around the city with a trailer in tow. I must have annoyed someone with my slow pace and when the individual passed me, he gave me the finger. While I missed the showing of the finger, Tibi did take notice, and asked me for the meaning of this gesture. I told him that that is the way we greet each other in Canada, and with a big smile we both proceeded by returning the kind gesture to the individual. I did explain to him afterwards the real intent of the message, as I did not want to be responsible for him walking around giving people the finger.

We loaded up the trailer with my futon bed, microwave and an old kitchen table. We were nuts. While that was all the furniture we had, it could have been replaced with about three hundred fifty dollars, and avoided all the hassles of moving it around. I most likely spent that much money just moving the furniture to Elliot Lake and back to Toronto.

During the move I noticed that Adriana had become very agitated and was starting to insist that I return the trailer and just leave the furniture in the apartment until we found a place to live in Toronto. I knew that something was wrong, so I went for a short walk alone with her, and explained that my landlord wanted the furniture out of the apartment by the end of the month, and we had nowhere else to store it. After about five minutes I finally got to the bottom of her concerns. She was afraid that once I moved all my belongings back north, I might decide to just stay there and never see her again. I could not believe what I was hearing! I took hold of both of her hands and looked into her eyes. I noticed that there were no tears in her eyes this time; she just seemed angry and almost scared. Holding her hands I told her that I loved her with all my heart and I would never leave her no matter what happened. She was still so insecure and so afraid that one day she would wake up and realize that I was not for real; that lurking in the shadows of my personality was some horrible and sinister side waiting patiently to hurt her when she least expected. A product of our environment, entrenched in patterns from the past, it so often seems that the more we learn about the world around us, based on our own unique life experiences, the less receptive we become to accepting the existence of alternatives. Jolted in the wake of what came before, with patience, love and understanding, I could only sway with her in the turbulence, knowing that in time the ripples from the past would dissipate into the depth, warmth and gentleness of the placid waters that now surrounded and engulfed her life, as she gradually opened her eyes to the possibility of alternatives.

On route back to Orangeville with my worldly belongings in tow, we had to make several stops, since my dad's car was starting to overheat. It was an older car, and as it turned out, the radiator was not quite up to the job of towing even a small trailer. When I arrived back in Orangeville, we had to take the car to Canadian Tire and have a new radiator installed before making the journey home again. With my graduation behind me, Adriana and I made plans to meet in mid June and spend the weekend in Parry Sound at a campsite. With our funds so low at the time, we decided that a weekend camping trip was a little more affordable than a weekend in a motel somewhere on Highway 69. With our plans made, Adriana returned to Toronto, where she lived with an older Romanian couple named Peter and Lucy, while she continued to work as a student nurse at Sunny Brook Hospital. I returned to my Parks and Recreation job in Elliot Lake.

Chapter 38

The Interview

Shortly after returning home, Adriana called to inform me that her sister had planned an engagement party for Sunday, June 10, which I was unable to attend because I was working the following day, and anyway, I was waiting for my next pay cheque to provide enough money to travel south and see her again. She was a little disappointed, but she did understand; however, the party plans continued despite my inability to attend. After wards, Adriana called to inform me about the new things she learned at our engagement party. The Romanian men at the party explained to Adriana that since I am from the north, I am spending my weekends having sex with women on the reservations, and then further explained to Adriana's family that they needed to break up this engagement. Otherwise Adriana would disappear into the north and never be seen again. As well, Lucy, her landlord at the time, explained that if I really was committed, I would have found some way to attend the party. She then presented Adriana with the very same lovely tea set that Adriana had given her as a gift only a few weeks before, out of appreciation for allowing her to live in her home for the summer. Lucy explained to Adriana that she was returning the gift as an engagement present, since she really had no use for the tea set in her home. After I assured Adriana that there was no validity to her guests' perspective on weekend excursions by northern boys she was reluctantly reassured of my commitment to her. I found the Romanian communities' perspective on Canadians to be somewhat disturbing but did my best to not let it bother me. Several weeks later I did see pictures from the engagement party, and found Adriana to be gorgeous. She was wore a lovely red dress and I wished so much that I could have been there with her.

With only a week to go before Adriana and I were to meet in Parry Sound, I received a call from the Future Shop head office in Toronto in response to a resume that I sent them. With this, plans for the weekend shifted a little. I booked Monday off work to attend the job interview, and made arrangements to meet Adriana Friday evening in Parry Sound. Instead of traveling south by motorbike, I borrowed my dad's car, since I needed to bring my suit along for the interview. Just before pulling out of the driveway Friday evening, Dad reminded me that the car was burning a little oil so I needed to check it at each fill-up. Mom and Dad knew that I was very low on cash, and even though they did not have much money, they loaned me their gas card so that I would have enough money to drive to and from the interview. Assuring Dad that I would check the oil, I headed down the highway with his Esso gas card in my pocket, and met Adriana at the Voyager Restaurant around 7 p.m. that evening.

After having a coffee we headed to Oastler Lake Provincial Park just south of Parry Sound and set up a small blue two-man pop tent and zipped our sleeping bags together. Before turning in for the night I lit my oil lamp and made a fire. Adriana had never been camping before. We truly enjoyed sitting beside each other on the bench of the picnic table cooking marshmallows and hotdogs over the fire. With dusk turned to night, the two of us sat on the bench talking and enjoying each other's company, as the fire cracked and popped before us, sending small orange flankers twirling and twisting into the dark starlit sky that blanketed the landscape around us. Adriana's complexion looked gorgeous as the soft flickering glow from the campfire chased shadows across her face, illuminating her in a most alluring manner. She always looked so beautiful in the soft glow of candlelight. Even today when we are camping with our two children William and Elizabeth, or sipping a martini late in the evening beside the soft glow of our living room woodstove, she looks so attractive and sexy with a combination of shadows and light from the flickering flames as they pass over and illuminate her facial features.

With the fire dying down and the chill of the night moving in around us, we crawled into our little tent and cuddled together under the sleeping bag, finding comfort in the gentle warmth of each other's body. Sometime in the early hours of the morning Adriana woke me with a gentle whisper in my ear, telling me that she could hear an animal snorting and breathing around our tent. I never camped much in provincial campgrounds, but rather opted for camping in the bush on fishing or hunting trips, and always slept with an ax beside my sleeping bag for protection. This was something that I always did, even back when I was camping as a teenager. Even though Adriana and I were in a provincial campground I continued with the practice. In all my years of camping, this was only one of three times when I woke in the night to take hold of the hickory axe handle that laid beside me. The first time was when I was a teenager on a weekend fishing trip with Nelson. We were camped on the shores of a secluded lake southeast of Elliot Lake, a half hour portage from the main highway. We woke in the early hours of the morning to the sound of an animal snorting and breathing on the outer side of the thin nylon walls that separated us from the creature that was investigating our campsite. Lying in my tent, I quietly moved my hand down the side of the sleeping bag and took hold of my hickory axe handle, holding it tight until I heard the sound of a rather large animal slip into the water and swim away. The third time I grabbed hold of my axe handle was during a caribou-hunting excursion to the Barrenland, just south of the Arctic Circle, where my hunting party camped over a hundred miles from the nearest road on the shore of a lake accessible only by air. After a weekend of hard work hunting caribou, I laid in my sleeping bag still chilled from the cold wet day in the field when a Barrenland grizzly, lured in by the scent of the fresh meat we had harvested, stocked our camp throughout the night and most of the following day. When its presence was first noticed, with nothing but a thin canvas wall between the predator and myself, I slipped my hand down the side of my sleeping bag, and took hold of my axe handle. By morning we had counted a total of five grizzlies and one tundra wolf that had stalked our camp during the night, and hunters formed a thin line firing warning shots to hold back the animals, often not more than twenty feet away. One of the grizzlies came so close that it actually pushed down some tent poles. When Adriana woke me that night in the Oastler Lake Provincial campground with her concern, stretching my hand out, I took hold of the ax handle as I carefully listened, only to realize that it was the gentleman in the next campsite snoring. Adriana and I both laughed and in a short while went back to sleep in the gentle warmth of each other's embrace.

The next morning we woke early and I cooked breakfast and made tea on my gas camp stove. The two of us sat at the picnic table and ate before taking down the campsite and showering. With our camping adventure behind us, we jumped in Dad's car and drove to Orangeville, arriving late Saturday afternoon. On Sunday evening I drove Adriana to the bus terminal so that she could return to Toronto for her shift at the hospital, and I spent the night at her sister's house. Early the next morning Mariana and I drove Dad's car into Toronto so that I could attend my interview at the Future Shop head office. Mariana knew Toronto well, and was able to guide me in and out of the city.

While I went for the interview, Mariana waited for me in the car. I was a little nervous sitting in the lobby, because until that day I had never participated in an interview. As I sat there that afternoon, I looked around and noticed that the other interviewees were much older than I, and obviously had much more life experience than

I. After waiting about a half hour, I was called into a little office where an East Indian man asked me questions about my past job experiences and my education and then explained to me that I could earn more money working as a salesperson at one of his stores than the university professors who I had studied under could ever hope to earn. About mid-way through the interview he asked me my age and then became very concerned and somewhat rude. He noted that since I was almost twenty-five years of age, there were obviously two years missing form my resume, as he looked square in my eyes and insisted that this interview would not continue for one second further until I accounted for those two years. He even suggested that perhaps I might actually be missing two years less a day from my resume, as I found myself shrinking in the chair under the weight of his stare feeling somewhat dumbfounded and assuring him that I had no idea what he was talking about. Becoming quite agitated, he further explained that since I would have graduated from high school at the age of eighteen that would allow me to complete an undergraduate program at the age of twenty-three, and since I was just about to turn twenty-five he demanded to know where I spent those two years that were not accounted for on my resume. It was at that point that I realized what he was talking about, as my face turned red with embarrassment and my heart began to sink. I had just graduated with honours from a Bachelor of Arts program with no accommodations, following the exact same degree requirements as my peers, even though I was one of those students in public school that most teachers did not feel would ever graduate, let alone complete a post secondary program. With shame, I looked into his eyes and informed him that as a child I failed grade one and then later as an adolescent I failed grade seven, and assured him that I could produce transcripts that clearly proved that I failed those two grades and in fact did not graduate from high school until I was twenty years of age, with my grade thirteen graduation taking place only two weeks before my twenty-first birthday. At this point he seemed to feel a little bad for being so judgmental, and assured me that the provision of a high school transcript would satisfy his need for verification. He then went on to explain that his only concern about me was that I came from a small northern town and would not have any concept of big business. Sitting before him feeling quite intimidated, I did not respond to this statement, but I do remember thinking to myself at the time that the two mining companies in my hometown rivaled the big three automakers in size, spending and profit, and for the most part, dwarfed his little operation. I left the interview somewhat ticked off, and when he called me at home a few days later to arrange an orientation date I declined the job offer.

With the interview behind me, I drove Mariana back to her home on the outskirts of Orangeville and headed north to Elliot Lake. As I was approaching the Voyager Restaurant just past the Parry Sound turn off around 10 p.m. I felt the engine of the car hesitate slightly, and then returned to normal operating conditions. It seemed odd, but I did not think much of it at the time, and in less than five minutes I pulled into the Voyageur Restaurant filled up with gas and sat down for a cup of warm coffee. When I returned to the car and started the engine I noticed that the oil light would not go out as usual, so I turned the engine off and checked the dipstick. To my amazement I could not see any oil on the stick, so I added a quart, and still did not see anything. After I put in three quarts of oil I noticed that the oil level had raised enough that it was registering the fact that I still needed one more quart of oil in the engine. In total the oil pan was down by four quarts of oil. It was at this point I realized that I had driven the car all the way to Toronto and almost back home without once checking the oil. I never did say anything to Dad about this, but afterwards he always complained that since my brother took the car to Sault Ste Marie one morning, it was never the same again because he drove the life out of it. Every time Dad mentioned this to me I felt a little uncomfortable and would change the topic. Nineteen years later, driving south on Highway 108 just north of Elliot Lake in my brother's pick-up truck, I asked him if he remembered how Dad used to complain about how he drove the life out of his car and the engine was never the same afterwards. Looking over at me from behind the wheel of his truck, he rolled his eyes and said, "I drove it once at 140 kilometers per hour and that apparently somehow wrecked his engine. I don't get it and I never lived it down!" Somewhat laughing I looked over at him and said that I always wondered if the engine problems Dad was experiencing had anything to do with the fact that I drove the car with no oil in the engine a little while before he took it on that fateful trip to the Sault. John laughed, looked over at me and said, "You bastard!"

Chapter 39

Prenuptial

A month before our wedding Adriana arrived in Elliot Lake in time for my twenty-fifth birthday and stayed with me for almost a week and a half, as we began the final preparations for our marriage. The evening that I was expecting her to arrive, John McDonald and James Kneen arrived at my door around seven o'clock to take me out for a few drinks. I turned them down, since Adriana was arriving in a few hours and I did not think that she would appreciate me sitting in a bar with my friends instead of meeting her at the bus stop. They were insisting on taking me out for a bachelor party, but I insisted equally that I could not attend. I was so excited about seeing Adriana that I could not even think of going out with the guys and having my family meet her instead of being there myself.

After much anticipation, Adriana arrived late in the evening on the Grey Coach. As soon as she stepped down from the bus we embraced in a passionate kiss as our bodies and lips gently pressed and molded into each other. As I held her, I told her how much I had missed her and how happy I was to have her in my arms again. But I remember being a little jealous and somewhat annoyed when she told me about some guy who wanted to kiss her on the bus. Apparently they were talking about lipstick and Adriana was explaining that she uses a certain type that doesn't rub off when you kiss. It seemed that the young man wanted to test this out with her, and she responded with something like, "No, no, no, you have to behave." Adriana was always such a flirt! Years later she told me that it used to annoy her a little that I never appeared jealous or concerned about her in any way, and in some ways I think she told me things like this to see if I really cared about her. At any rate, I always play my cards close to my chest, and whether I showed it or not, I remember not being too impressed when I heard about the incident.

It is hard to believe that I was only twenty-five and Adriana was still twenty-one years old. At the time we thought we were so grownup, but looking back we were still so young and knew so little. Adriana was going into her third year of nursing, and I had just completed my B.A with no employment prospects, no apartment in Toronto as of yet, and the only furnishings we had consisted of an old twelve inch black and white television, the kitchen table and chairs from my apartment in Waterloo, and a narrow single size futon bed – all stored in my parents' back shed. We really had nothing more than a motorbike and a few hundred dollars between us. Looking back it was really scary just how little we started with, and yet at the time the only thing I could think of was how happy I was that in less than a month Adriana and I would be together for the rest of our lives. It seemed like we were always saying good-bye, and now with the wedding only a few weeks away I would no longer be lonely. Adriana would be with me all the time.

While in Elliot Lake that week, Adriana arranged for the purchase of our marriage license at the town hall. I remember that afternoon very well. Working as a summer student for Parks and Recreation I was tending to the gardens in the boulevard across from the fire station when I saw Adriana and one of my sisters walking into the town hall to arrange to purchase the license. I called out to her and she waved at me as she walked into the main lobby. By the time she was done I had moved on to another garden elsewhere in town.

As well, that week we went to a small jewelry store beside the old Hudson Bay, and purchased our wedding rings. We had very little money at the time, and had to settle for a simple ten-karat set that cost about one hundred dollars. I remember the store had more fancy rings and even if we could have afforded one of the more flashy sets, I still think that I would have purchased the simple ring set that we selected. A wedding ring is a symbol of love and commitment between two people, and a simple plain ten-karat set can say that every bit as clearly as a eighteen karat set with fancy inlayed white gold over yellow. I can still see the two of us standing in the small jewelry store trying on our matching set of rings, and thinking to myself that in just a little over a month we will be married, as I glanced over at Adriana feeling so secure and loved and looking so forward to dedicating the rest of my life to her. I was so in love with her and still could not really believe that I found such a beautiful person to share the rest of my life with.

While Adriana always seemed to manage to break something while visiting my home, my parents never seemed to mind because everyone loved her so much. She had a beautiful personality and was always so willing to help with the dishes as well as the cooking. My family admired her hard work ethic and her pleasant personality. She never had a mean or distasteful word for anyone and just seemed happy all the time. Later that week as I sat in the kitchen repairing the vegetable crisper handle in the fridge that she broke while making a salad for supper, my mother told me that Adriana had talked with my sisters about just how lucky she felt to be marrying such a special, caring and kind man. My mother told me that both Adriana and I were very lucky because we both appreciated each other so much. She also told me that in a conversation, my grandma Underhill had expressed hope that Adriana and I would be happy together. Grandma told Mom, "A marriage is like tying a knot in the tongue that your teeth can't undo." Mom assured Grandma that the marriage between Adriana and me would last because we just seemed so right for each other and really loved each other.

That week I also applied for five days off work in order to get married, and my supervisor reluctantly gave approval. He told me that summer students don't have any leave with or without pay, but they would make an exception in this case, since I clearly needed time off to attend my own wedding. The rest of the week was spent driving around on our two-toned baby blue 750 Virago, drinking coffee at Peachy's with Dad, one visit to the Algo Inn and a lot of time together alone whenever we could find a little privacy, even if only for a few minutes in my bedroom.

The weekend following my birthday Adriana and I hopped on our bike and headed south to Orangeville, via Manitouland Island. As usual, in preparation for the trip I stuffed our clothing into the leather saddlebags that hung on either side of the passenger seat. The bags were small, and our rain gear consumed half of the luggage space. To make matters worse, Adriana always traveled with a few more clothes than could comfortably fit into the saddlebags. Yet no matter how much clothing we traveled with, I somehow always managed to make it all fit by rolling everything into small tight little balls to stuff into the two compartments. Adriana would watch me accomplish this feat with a certain sour look about her, almost as if she was saying to her self, "Okay, this will take a while to iron out!" In our riding leather, we pulled out of my parents' driveway, with Mom and Dad both waving. Unfortunately we left a little too late and as we approached South Bay Mouth with darkness all around us a host of cars almost blinding me with a continuous stream of headlights traveled north on Highway 6. Since South Bay Mouth was the end of the road, I knew that this meant that the ferry had arrived and was now preparing to load up for the return trip across the bay. I hit the gas a little harder in order to make the ferry before it sailed into the night. We were a little too far out of town and arrived just in time to watch it sail out of the harbour into the darkness of the night. It was a romantic experience as Adriana and I stood beside our bike on the edge of the wharf looking out over the darkness of the bay watching the silhouette of the ship dotted in small white lights sailing into the darkness of a summer evening. The chill of night was starting to settle across the island and into our bones as we decided on our next move. There were no motels in town, and we did not want to travel back to Little Current. However, with few options we headed back up Highway 6 in hopes of finding a roadside motel. After driving a short distance out of town we came upon a small campground on the outskirts of South Bay Mouth that advertised both cabins and campsites. We drove in and to our luck we rented a small one-room cabin for the night. It was very simple, with just a double bed pushed up against the wall and a small kitchen table with two chairs. We were starving at the time, as we had not eaten anything since noon, and it was now ten in the evening. The lady working at the front desk felt sorry for us and sold us a can of tuna and four slices of bread. We had no cash with us at the time and had to purchase the food on my credit card. We were so hungry and so grateful for the food.

As Adriana was about to lay beside me in bed, she took out a pocket camera and snapped a picture of me. Just as she pointed the camera, I pulled the blanket over my head. Nineteen years later I found that picture in an old album in Mom's basement hiding behind a picture of some cabins lining the shoreline near South Bay Mouth – pictures that Adriana took from the ferry the following day. I think that I hid that picture of myself under the blankets years ago and forgot about it. As I pulled the picture from the album, somewhat reminiscing in the past, I noticed the inscription that Adriana wrote on the back of the photo:

> Mike's hiding under the covers – He doesn't want me to take a picture of his pretty face. I love you very much. I'll never stop loving you. It was a wonderful and romantic trip and cruise with a very special man. - South Bay Mouth in a cabin at 11:00 pm on July 6, 1990 – Friday evening. (Adriana Sas, July 1990)

I remember being a little annoyed with her at the time for taking a picture of me in bed, but looking at it many years later and reading the inscription she wrote on the back, my heart melted as I recalled just how much she always loved me and how lucky I am to have found her. No person on this Earth could have loved me as much as she did and still does. In fact, as much as we were in love twenty years ago, we are a thousand times more in love today. I am so happy that she snapped that quick little picture of me under the blankets so long ago and wrote that beautiful inscription on the back. As I sat alone in my mother's basement years later looking at that picture and reading the inscription for the first time, my heart swelled with love for Adriana. With a lump in my throat, I quietly reminisced in the innocence, beauty and romance of that evening that we shared in the twilight of our youth so many years ago on the south shore of the Manitouland Island.

The next morning we arose early, and headed back to the ferry. When we arrived we were at the back of a long line of traffic, but were quickly led to the front. This was a routine that Adriana and I were used to, since ferry workers always allowed bikes to enter the ship first, so it did not really matter when we arrived, so long as we were there before the ferry set sail. Once I tied the bike down, we headed to the kitchen for breakfast and then spent time on the deck taking pictures and looking out over the water. An elderly gentleman noticed us taking pictures of each other and offered to take a photo of us together. It is one of the few pictures we ever had of the two of us on one of our motorbike adventures and perhaps the only picture we have of Adriana and me together on the ferry. Twenty years later that picture of Adriana and me in our leather jackets and tight fitting acid-wash jeans hangs on our bedroom wall as a quiet and gentle reminder of simpler days when we were carefree, young and newly in love.

As the ferry made its final approach to the dock, I untied my bike, and we put on our helmets and mounted, as we waited for the signal to move out. The final approach to the dock was always a little tricky, since I had to keep the bike steady under us as it swayed back and forth a little with the movement of the boat. Adriana would always hold me a little tighter during the docking procedure, with her arms wrapped tightly around my upper body. Once the ferry was docked, I fired up the engine, Adriana gave me a little squeeze and we roared out of the opening at the end of the ferry and down Highway 6, past Owen Sound and on to Orangeville. I needed to be back to work for Monday morning, so we had only Saturday and part of Sunday together before I had to return to Elliot Lake. Adriana could not come back with me, since she had to stay in Orangeville and help prepare for our wedding. It was an exciting time filled with anticipation.

Chapter 40

The Honeymoon Suite

With still no apartment lined up in Toronto for the fall, and since I had to work until mid September in Elliot Lake, we agreed to live at my parents' house for the month following our marriage. So on my return to Elliot Lake, I decided that since we did not have our own apartment to go to after our marriage, I would at least paint and clean up my bedroom downstairs. With the help of my family, I moved out all of the furniture, painted the walls and cleaned the windows. Cleaning the windows was a big job, since they were old and held into place with a series of connectors and screws. I remember looking at a series screws and matching holes as I was trying to reinstall the windows and in frustration commented that I did not know which hole to screw the window attachments back into. My sister Kim picked up on this comment and turned it into something else. I remember thinking at the time, "Okay, funny, very funny," and continued with the job of preparing our little honeymoon suite in my parents' basement. The last part of the job involved moving the bunk bed set to an upstairs bedroom and bringing down a double bed from my sister's room, so that Adriana and I would not have to argue over who got the top bunk.

Since I missed my bachelor party with John and James the week before, John McDonald and I went out to a beer fest at the Central Arena on the other side of town. In those days Elliot Lake was still a rough-and-tough mining town, although not quite as rough and tough as the boom years of the early 1980's. After a few mugs of beer, John and I walked home around midnight. We went to John's house first, and then I was about to continue on to my house alone when a police car pulled up and two offices got out, walked over to me and demanded to know my name and where I was coming from. I told them who I was, where I came from and where I was heading. The officer then informed me that he had a report of two young men chasing girls near Collin's Hall, a community center about a mile up the road. I assured the officer that my friend and I were not a party to that incident. As we were talking, one of the offices walked close to me in an attempt to be intimidating, so I moved in closer to him, to let him know that I was not feeling threatened. As I was talking to him, his partner moved around to my back and I knew things were about to take a bad turn, but there was no way I was going to back down from these guys. They were bullies and I was going to stand my ground! Several years before this I had earned a brown belt in karate and was somewhat confident that I could at least hold my own. As things came to a critical point, my friend, who was watching the incident unfold from his living room window, walked outside and simply asked, "What's the problem?" I looked over at John and said, "They are accusing us of chasing girls!" John McDonald looked over at the two officers and said, "It was not us." Standing only an inch from my nose and on the verge of physical contact with me, the officer put both of his hands in the air, backed down and said, "We must be mistaken." The two officers got in their car and drove off. I think the fact that John McDonald's father was the deputy chief of police helped a little in this situation. Even so, perhaps I could have handled the situation a little better, but back then Elliot

Lake was pretty rough and its police force had to be even rougher. I remember during my high school years hearing of odd students being caught raising a little hell in the evening, and how the police would take them to the old beach in the late hours of the night and leave them beaten on the lakeshore. While taking a grade 12 law class, one of the town police officers came to talk to us. He openly admitted that this practice does occur once in a while, and made a certain plea for understanding, since police officers are people too, and like anyone will experience a bad day once and a while. As a teenager, even though I was not a trouble-maker and never had any conflict with the law, I used to have a reoccurring nightmare of the Elliot Lake Town Police chasing me through town, as I made every effort to escape by finding my way off the streets and into the bush. In this dream, every time I thought that I found a route to the bush, an impenetrable green wall of trees or a fence that I could not scale would confront me. Back then I promised myself that if I ever fell victim to their abuse I would go down fighting. However, looking back, perhaps a week before my wedding was not the best time to make a stand, and as the years passed, I tried to become a little more selective about which hills were actually worth dying on.

The week passed quickly, and on the wet, drizzling Saturday morning of July 28, 1990 I left my parents' home early, riding my baby blue VX 750 Virago south to Orangeville. With my red and white rain-suit covering my University of Waterloo jacket and my blue jeans I drove south on Highway 108, turned east on Highway 17 and south on Highway 6 to South Bay Mouth, were I caught the ferry across the bay. During the crossing I met a couple in their mid-fifties driving a Goldwing. They were retired and were biking around for the summer. They told me that since it was so wet outside and they had no real agenda, they were going to stop at a roadside motel and wait out the weather for a day or two. I remember explaining to them that I was heading south for my wedding in one week's time, and was looking forward to seeing my fiancée. Once on the other side of the bay I continued south on Highway 6 until I reached Highway 89 east to Shelburne and south on the third line to Adriana's sister's home.

When I arrived at the house, I was wet and tired, and just enjoyed sitting at the dinning room table with Adriana and her brother-in-law John. There was lots of alcohol in the house, since we were stocked for an open bar at the wedding. As we sat there that afternoon we dipped into the Captain Morgan spiced rum and coke, while the kitchen was occupied by a number of older Romanian women who were busy making enough cabbage-rolls for the near one hundred and fifty guests we were expecting at our wedding the following weekend. As I made my way to the kitchen for a glass of water, a few of the woman took the opportunity to explain to me the difference between Canadian and Romanian marriages. Looking somewhat like an old Italian widow, this older woman in a long black dress who could speak a little English turned to me and sternly said in broken English, "Canadians divorce, Romanians no divorce." The other women who could speak English a little better joined the conversation and further explained to me that Canadians do not really take marriages very seriously in contrast to Romanians, who respect their wedding vows and never get divorced. In that short conversation I learned that Canadians do not take marriages very seriously, are not very romantic or caring, lack a certain level of intelligence and sophistication, are for the most part lazy, soft and over weight, like to drink a lot of beer, and apparently do not speak the Queen's English. I remember thinking at the time that they must have fallen in with a dreadful group of people during their short stay in this country, and I hoped that they would have the opportunity to meet some of the more respectful, hardworking, and honorable Canadians that make up the majority of the population of this fine country. At any rate, the women did make a great batch of cabbage-rolls. But more to the point, I was about to marry the most beautiful girl in the entire world – someone whom I loved and adored – and with that in my back pocket I did not really care about their perception of myself or my fellow countrymen.

As the week progressed Adriana and I made one attempt at finding an apartment in Toronto for the fall. We were getting a little desperate, since we needed a place to live in less than a month when she returned to her nursing program. Armed with a Toronto newspaper with a few ads circled, we began the long process of securing residence. Unfortunately, with Adriana being a student and me with no work yet, we were having a difficult time finding anyone who would let us rent. As we became more desperate, we checked out a basement apartment some distance from her college. It was a dingy little place with a low ceiling, but at the same time we needed to find a place soon. Adriana told the lady that we would really like to rent the apartment, and the response shocked us. The lady told us to submit a resume with references and she would get back to us if we made the short list. I remember thinking to myself, "To hell with this. I am not submitting a resume and participating in an interview for a basement apartment."

Making our way back to the subway we were a little discouraged, as the reality set in that finding a place to live was going to prove a little more difficult than we initially thought and time was running out. As we stood on the platform talking, a subway train came to a stop and before we had time to board, we heard someone call our names. We looked down the platform to see Sanford and Caroline emerging from one of the cars. They were in the city for the day and catching a train back to their car, which they left at one of the malls on the north end of the city. En route back to their car, they noticed Adriana and me standing on the platform. We caught the next train with them and they gave us a ride back to Orangeville. Adriana and I took a seat in the very same car that we rode in the day we first met each other eighteen months previous. It was kind of ironic, but we actually had the same seating arrangement, with Adriana sitting just behind me on the passenger side of the car. Meeting Caroline and Sanford was a pleasant surprise, since we were planning on catching a bus back to town and would have to find a ride to the third line with someone.

At any rate, Mariana helped us solve the apartment issue about two weeks following the wedding. She discovered that a Romanian lady was moving out of a bachelor apartment on Raglan Avenue near the corner of St. Clair and Bathurst. She met with the Hungarian superintendent, explained that Adriana was a nurse and I was an engineer, both with good solid employment, and slipped him a one hundred dollar bill to secure the apartment. By hook or crook we had landed our first apartment, and Adriana managed to get into it and painted it pink from wall to wall about a week before I arrived. Pink was her favouite colour. Once it was fully furnished it actually didn't look too bad with our black and white twelve-inch television, an old wobbly kitchen table and chairs and our single size futon bed off to the side. It was a very humble start, but we were together and that was all that really seemed to matter at the time. Nevertheless, at the time, with the wedding only a few days away, the lack of proper living accommodations was still weighing heavily as we returned to Orangeville that evening, somewhat discouraged by our failed attempt to find an apartment.

As the week moved on we had other affairs to attend to, such as getting the tuxedos and taking in all of the pre-marriage parties. As we were preparing for our wedding, Adriana and I had our first real argument Tuesday afternoon. I am sure there was a little more to it, yet it started off with Adriana getting very frustrated translating a conversation between her mother and me, when Adriana finally told me in frustration that maybe I needed to find a Canadian girl so I would not require a translator to communicate with the family. The argument seemed to carry on for the whole day, finally ending with the two us having a reconciliation once we got away from everyone and could talk in private for a while.

The following day, on Wednesday afternoon, we attended our final marriage preparation meeting with the Anglican minister in Shelburne. The first meeting with him had been sometime in the winter, followed by a second meeting in the spring and a final meeting with him just before the wedding. The meetings gradually over time went from why we wanted to get married, to how much we knew of each other, our plans for the future and finally preparations for the actual wedding. To date, the meetings had not gone very well, which was perhaps in some small way my fault, since during one of our previous sessions I had referred to the minister as a very fine spiritual leader of a nice little cult organization. I sometimes have a knack for saying the wrong thing at the wrong time.

Lynn and Andre arrived that evening. My cousin John drove

me to the airport to meet them, and since we had no hotel rooms booked for another night, they returned to Mariana's house with me and slept in the living room on a pull out couch.

I, as well, was still staying at Adriana's sister's house, and that night Adriana and I slept together for the last time before becoming husband and wife. There were a lot of people in the house at the time, and Adriana and I actually ended up sharing a room for the night. I slept on a single size bed in her niece's bedroom, while she slept on the floor beside my bed with her niece and nephew. Sometime after midnight when everyone was sound asleep I awoke to find Adriana sliding into bed beside me. We quietly kissed and made love for the last time before our wedding. Holding each other with quiet anticipation of what was to come, we fell asleep for a little while. Sometime before the light of the new day broke Adriana quietly slipped back to the floor and slept with the two children.

Nelson arrived Thursday afternoon for the wedding in his new blue quarter-ton Nissan, and that night, two days before our wedding, we went to a local bar called the Rusty Nail and partied with family and friends. Tibi, Daniel, Caroline, Sanford, Nelson, Adriana and I all sat at a table on the balcony. We drank, ate and partied all night. Lynn and Andre did not attend, since they took my motorbike into Toronto for the day to visit some friends and did not get back until later that evening. Sometime around midnight Adriana, Tibi and Daniel returned to Mariana's house, while Nelson and I took one of the three rooms that Mom booked at the Orangeville Motel. When we got there I noticed that Andre and Lynn had already returned, since they had parked the bike outside of the motel. I thought of getting my helmets and key back from them, but it was late and I was ready to retire to my room. As I was about to walk through the doorway to my room, I looked back and noticed Nelson completely drunk and trying to open his truck door to go for a ride. I walked over to him and asked him just what the hell he thought he was doing and told him to give me the keys. He started laughing, holding the keys away from me and insisting on taking the truck for a spin. After about a minute of trying to reason with him I said, "Do whatever you want," and walked into the room. He made some comment like, "Friends don't let friends drink and drive. You should have tried a little harder to stop me," as he followed me into the hotel room. I responded by simply saying, "What ever," and went to bed. We were both a little too hammered to be carrying on any level of intelligent conversation at the time, let alone this nonsense.

Friday morning Nelson and I picked up Caroline and Adriana, and we met Lynn and Andre for breakfast at Harvey's Restaurant. This was the start of the last day that I could call Adriana my girlfriend, as we sat there that morning only thirty hours from our marriage.

We were really trying to set Nelson up with my cousin Caroline. She seemed to like him, but he had no interest in her. Unfortunately, everyone except Nelson thought that they were a perfect couple. After breakfast we went over to the hall to help get the tables and chairs ready for the reception and then went over to the church for our marriage rehearsal. When it came time to kiss the bride Adriana and I were a little nervous and only pecked each other on the lips. The minister stopped the practice and said, "Come on, you can do a little better than that! Show a little passion!" He actually made Adriana and me practice our marriage kiss several times before he felt we were demonstrating enough passion, and the following day during the wedding ceremony when it came time for the kiss he actually commented that Adriana and I practiced for some time to get it just right.

Following the rehearsal we all gathered for a big celebration at my Uncle Herman's house. That evening at the party, Nelson and I were in competition to see who could drink the most potent Prairie Fire, a contest that Nelson won, much to the concern of my Aunt Dorothy. Aunt Dorothy actually pulled me aside and informed me that if Nelson did not stop drinking I will not have a best man at the wedding the following day.

Adriana was wearing a beautiful red dress that night and looked stunning. However, she had a little disagreement with her nephew Alex, who himself was having a little difficulty accepting the upcoming marriage. Both he and his sister had always been very close with Adriana, and our relationship was coming between them.

Adriana was feeling quite hurt and was in tears as a result of the disagreement, so we went for a short walk hand in hand.

During this walk I expressed some disappointment in myself for mixing Nelson a highly potent Prairie Fire, and felt that I should have demonstrated a little more responsibility and good judgment. Adriana, for the most part, agreed with me. We were both a little nervous about the wedding the following day. While we did not realize it at the time, that walk was our last moments together as boyfriend and girlfriend before becoming husband and wife. As we returned to my uncle's house we kissed under the cover of darkness and parted ways for the night, knowing that the next time our lips would touch we would be husband and wife, with a commitment to dedicating the rest of our life to each other. As I held her in my arms I looked into her eyes and felt myself to be the luckiest man on the planet, knowing that in less that twenty hours this beautiful young woman, only twenty-one years of age, was to become my wife. After parting ways that warm summer starlit evening, I did not see her again until she walked towards me in church the following day wearing her beautiful long white wedding gown. She was so beautiful.

Chapter 41

Wedding Day

The morning of Saturday August 4th Adriana prepared for our marriage at her sister's home, while I remained at my uncle's house learning to play Ucer, a card game that I never really seemed to master.

Adriana and I were married in the Anglican Church in Shelburne, Ontario. This was several years before we actually converted to the Roman Catholic faith, and at the time I was hoping that our marriage in the Anglican Church would be a form of healing for my family and eventually help to bring my family back to the church. In fact, when Adriana and I eventually did formally convert to Roman Catholicism several years later Adriana and I refused to allow the priest to marry us in the Catholic Church, even though that was a formal requirement for conversion. Eventually the priest dropped the issue because he knew that it was a make-or-break deal for Adriana and me. The marriage and the vows that we exchanged twenty years ago were sacred, and I would never do anything that denied the validity of our marriage or the sanctity of the vows that we exchanged that day. However, eighteen years later we did renew our vows, when we arrived at mass one Sunday morning in the community of Behchoko in the Northwest Territories to discover that all married couples in the parish were to stand together during mass and renew their marriage vows in the Tlicho language. So, there with our two children, my sister Nancy, and my mother-in-law under the roof of an open-air mass we reaffirmed our commitment to one another.

About an hour before our marriage Nelson drove me to the church, where he and I waited in the basement until it was time for the ceremony to begin. I was so nervous! On the way to the church we passed the two-storey white and orange hotel where my family was lodging on Highway 10 near Orangeville. My mother and father actually paid for three rooms at the hotel for three nights so that my family would have a place to stay. As we drove past the hotel I saw my mother quickly moving across the second floor balcony from one room to another, as everyone prepared to attend the ceremony.

As the ceremony began, I remember standing at the front of the church and watching as Adriana walked towards me with her mother on one side and her brother-in-law on the other, led by Dawna as the flower girl and my cousin Caroline as the maid of honour. I remember being amazed at how beautiful Adriana looked in her wedding dress.

Adriana was always very emotional, especially during happy occasions, and this is something that I have always loved about her. As we stood at the front of the church alone with the minister taking our vows, Adriana started crying a little. I remember looking over at her as we stood side by side and said, "It's alright," as I gave her hand a gentle reassuring squeeze.

Following the ceremony we had our pictures taken in a nearby park. Then John Moga drove us to the reception hall in a rented grey New Yorker. The reception was beautiful. My parents and brother got lost on the way to the reception, so we waited as André went looking for them, and finally found them at the hotel. They knew that someone would come looking for them and thought that the hotel would be a good place to be found.

Since pink was Adriana's favourite colour, she decided to have a large helium-filled pink and white balloon arrangement about forty-five feet long that arched behind our table. Throughout the evening we danced a lot and kissed every time the guests started tapping their wine glasses with a knife or fork.

There was an odd little Romanian tradition involving youth stealing and hiding the shoes of the bride, and the groom or best man was supposed to pay the children for their return. Alex had learned of this tradition and decided that he would make an easy fifty dollars that evening. He grabbed one of Adriana's shoes just as we were about to walk to the dance floor for our first dance as husband and wife. He ran out the door with it, returning in a short while to inform Nelson that he wanted fifty dollars. Nelson and I were willing to pay up to twenty-five dollars, but felt that a fifty dollar ransom was abusing the tradition and spirit of the moment. Today I earn over fifty dollar an hour, so his ransom would not be such a big deal; however, at the time I was only earning six dollars an hour and it took me almost two days of hard labour under the hot sun and pouring rain to earn that kind of cash. After a lengthy discussion between Alex, Nelson and myself, we finally made Alex show us the location of the shoe and refused to pay him anything at the time. We found the shoe in the bushes at the front of the reception hall. The following day I gave Alex fifteen dollars to honour the tradition. After returning the shoe to its proper place on Adriana's slender sexy foot, we walked hand in hand to the dance floor and danced our first dance as husband and wife that evening to the song, Tonight I Celebrate My Love For You, by Gloria Loring.

Adriana and I were both a little nervous and did not eat nor drink much during the evening. However, unlike many newlyweds, we stayed at the reception until the late hours of the night before retiring to a local inn. We wanted to enjoy as much of the celebration as possible, and Adriana was having so much fun dancing.

Following the reception, we took a twenty-minute taxi ride to the Hockley Inn. In fact Nelson paid the taxi driver forty-five dollars, as his last duty that evening as best man. After we checked in and arrived at our room I picked up Adriana in my arms and carried her into our room, where we noticed that the small bottle of champagne we were expecting was not waiting for us. Adriana made a quick call to the front desk, and a bottle arrived in a short while, with apologies. We sat on the bed together with Adrianna still in her beautiful white wedding gown and I in my black long-tailed tuxedo as we had a toast to our new life together before consummating our marriage.

The following day we returned to her sister's house to open presents and to continue with the celebration. In addition to gifts, we accumulated three thousand dollars in cash, bringing our total cash reserves to about three thousand and fifty dollars. We even went back to the reception hall late in the afternoon to help clean the building. As we were helping to clean the reception hall, Adriana and I took down the long white and pink balloon arrangement that arched over our table the night before and moved the entire arrangement, completely intact, outside. We did not have the heart to break the balloons so we released it into the air. To our amazement, the entire arrangement that consisted of three rows of balloons, lifted into the air and floated off into the sky in a long endless wave, almost mystical – much like an ancient dragon flying off to some unknown and mysterious destination. As we stood alone in the gravel parking lot of the Mono Mills Reception Hall, hand in hand on our first day as husband and wife, we looked over an almost infinite spread of green fields. We watched the balloon arrangement disappear in a seemingly endless wave; and as it floated off into the distance that warm, summer mid-afternoon, its direction was uncertain, like the destination of our own life together. We wondered where the winds of fate would take it, and us.

Chapter 42

Honeymoon

I had to return to work that Tuesday so we were unable to have a real honeymoon at the time. We planned on settling for one night together on Manitoulin Island in transit home on our motorbike. Unfortunately I had loaned my motorbike to André the day before the wedding, and he accidentally dropped the key for the bike in my bother's car. Thus, the day following our marriage, I had to push the bike about seven miles up hill from the Orangeville Hotel on Highway 10 back to my uncle's house on the other side of town.

Our travel plans for the return trip to Elliot Lake were thus switched from a motorbike ride to a Grey Coach ticket. As Adriana and I sat beside each other on the return bus trip we were just happy being together as newlyweds, only two days following our wedding. When we walked onto the bus in Toronto hand in hand, we were very saddened to look around for a double seat, only to realize that Adriana would have to sit at the back of the bus and I somewhere in the middle. Standing in the center of the bus, we kissed each other and gradually parted ways for our seats, as her hand slowly slid out of mine. I was sitting half way across the bus from her and we looked almost starry-eyed at each other, when the woman sitting beside me finally said, "Would you like me to move so that your girlfriend can sit with you?" I told her that I would appreciate that very much and the seat exchange was made. Now side-by-side Adriana and I snuggled into each other for the long eight-hour bus ride home.

We arrived home late on the evening of Monday, August 6, 1990, and found Dad sitting alone in the kitchen smoking a cigarette and drinking a cup of tea. I remember yawning a few times and trying to gently nudge Adriana along, but Dad just kept talking, and we seemed stuck in the kitchen, unable to move on for the night. Adriana and I talked with him for a little while, until I finally said that I was tired and went to bed. Then I lay in bed listening to Dad and Adriana talking for another ten minutes. I could tell that she wanted to join me, but did not want to be rude. After a short while, Adriana joined me in the honeymoon suite.

Chapter 43

Merging Paths

We have come so far and grown so close since that cool crisp autumn day over twenty years ago when we first met in the twilight of our youth, catching each other's eye for a brief second and exchanging a simple greeting that consisted of nothing more than saying "hi" to each other, as Adriana moved her long slender gorgeous body around me and settled into the back seat of Uncle Herman's car.

It is overpowering and awe-inspiring to look back and reflect on how far we have come and how close we have become since that first simple encounter so many years ago. We have shared many wonderful experiences over the past twenty-one years, and yet as the years slipped by and time moved on, the days, months and years started to blend together until it became difficult to remember the order and time of so many special and wonderful moments that we shared. These are life-altering experiences, both great and tragic, that seem to stand out for an eternity – like the day we first met, our first date, our wedding day, the birth of our children, my father's passing and my first job in Big Trout Lake. Then there are other more subdued experiences that capture a moment in time, embodied in a feeling or even an aura of something special and meaningful that often slips into lost memories that fade with time. These are special moments, like the time we parked our motorbike under an overpass to escape a downpour. We parked the bike on the side of the road under the overpass, and sat on the concrete slab under the bridge side by side with our arms around each other, leaning into each other's body for warmth and comfort as we watched the cars moving up and down the highway while we waited for the rain to stop. Then there was that cold January evening in 1996 when we sat in a dark corner of the Red Dog Inn sharing a candlelit dinner after a long day on the highway en-route to Big Trout Lake. That year was the last Christmas we shared with my Dad before his death. As we sat there I could not take my eyes off Adriana. The soft flickering glow from the candle chasing shadows across her face seemed to illuminate her completion in a soft glow. I could not stop thinking about her that evening and the child that she carried in her, as we shared a late evening supper, knowing that our life was about to become so much more enriched with the expected birth of our first child in eight short months.

As the years passed we grew closer together, as we opened our lives to share with our two children. The world has changed over the last twenty years and we have moved along with those changes. I don't think that it really sank in for us until our nineteenth anniversary, when we returned to the restaurant that we went to on our first date over twenty years ago and sat at the same table in the restaurant. It was actually the first time we had returned there since that first date, and we noticed that the restaurant had been renovated sometime over the years, altering its dim candlelit almost-sixties décor to a more colourful, open and brighter atmosphere. The restaurant was not the only thing that had changed. We were a little heavier and slightly greyer than we were twenty years ago – with two beautiful children, a house, cars, investments and careers. We were no longer the same two people that we were twenty years ago, with not much more to our names than the clothing on our backs, a clock radio, an old motorbike and real dark hair that didn't require dyes to help maintain our youthful appearance. Even with all the changes around us, as we sat there that afternoon and looked across the table into each other's eyes, we fell back to a simpler time when we first met and fell in love so many years ago in the twilight of our youth.

Our lives and the world today seem so much more complicated. As we drove through Kitcherner-Waterloo that afternoon, we noticed that so much had changed over the past twenty years. The Waterloo movie theater, where we spent so many Friday nights holding hands and kissing in the back row, is no longer a theater. Even the Bombshelter had undergone a slight renovation, not much, but still just enough to feel different. As we sat in the Bombshelter that afternoon drinking a cup of green tea and worrying a little that the parking meter would expire before we returned to our vehicle, we looked around and realized that most of the people in that university pub were not even born when we partied there over twenty years ago. Adriana pointed out a young girl in the pub frantically typing on a laptop. You could tell she was desperately pumping out an essay under the pressure of an ever-nearing due date, as we both quietly agreed that we wouldn't want to be doing it all over again. Even that young girl typing frantically symbolized such a change in the times. When I completed my Master's Degree, I wrote all my essays and even my thesis on paper with a pencil, and paid someone to type for me on a real typewriter. For me in those days, cut and paste actually involved a pair of scissors and some tape, as I edited my papers by moving paragraphs around to make a stronger and more consistent essay. My research came from books in a library and writing was done on paper with a pencil, and I used to carry all of my research notes in my backpack. The internet did not even exist then. Now everyone has a laptop and portable internet connections. After leaving the Bombshelter that afternoon, we even stopped our pickup truck outside of 56 Helene Crescent, and we sat in our truck on the side of the road in silence for what seemed like an eternity looking at the basement apartment where we first made love and shared so many wonderful and heartwarming weekends together over twenty years ago.

In coming together, we have enriched each other's lives so much more than words can ever begin to explain. Even though we often would like to stop time and hold onto special moments, we never really can, because life moves on and we change with time. Nevertheless, ours is a story that needs to be remembered as we pause once in a while freeing ourselves from the boundaries of time and space to reminiscence in forgotten and faded memories from the past, and even if only for a brief moment, we can slip back to a simpler time and reflect on the many wonderful life experiences that we have shared when we were young, newly in love and full of youthful innocence and adventure.

My dear Adriana, I love you so much more than you will ever know.

With All My Love,
Michael

Appendix

The following is a section of the story from chapter 34, the "Weary Rose" that includes a prank that I included for my sister Nancy. Nancy's encouragement and help with editing and feedback was invaluable as I placed the many pieces of this story together from memories that were over two decades old. Over the years, Nancy was always so good at catching me in some wild pranks, and I just could not resist the opportunity to finally get one over on her. As the words to follow unfolded before her eyes, her heart came to her throat in disbelief and horror at the mere thought of the terrible misfortune that had befallen poor Adriana, only to learn at the end of this transcript that the terrifying events described below never really happened. Even after learning the truth, she was actually shaken for several days following her experience reading this chapter. After inserting the following events into my manuscript I patiently waited several weeks, until she finally found the time to read the updates that I submitted to her. Late one evening while sitting at the kitchen table with Adriana, our son William and our daughter Elizabeth, I received a phone call from Nancy. As I put the phone to my ear I heard the words, "You're a jerk." I simply responded by saying, "The Weary Rose," to which she replied a cold and shaken,

"Yes," and suggested that she may insert a few surprises of her own into the manuscript.

Alone again with Adriana and her wilting rose now trimmed in a blackish touch of frostbite on he edges, I walked Adriana back to the Subway station, before catching my bus north. She wanted to remain at the bus station and see me off, but I was afraid to have her walk alone to the subway so late in the evening, so I convinced her to let me walk her to the subway; otherwise, I would have worried all the way home. On the way to the subway I was very conscious of the direction I was walking, so that I could find my way back to the bus terminal. Once at the top of the stairs leading to the underground subway, Adriana and I kissed good-bye, as she slowly pulled away from me and walked down the stairs. It seemed we were always parting ways.

On my way back to the bus terminal, I recognized the corner where we met the elderly gentleman only an hour ago. Looking up, I laughed to myself, taking note that we met him on the corner of Francis and Dejarda. With Adriana on my mind, I made my way back to the bus terminal and boarded the coach for the long ride north. I looked forward to the following weekend when I could take Adriana in my arms and kiss her again. As I took my seat in the bus and felt very lonely for Adriana, I could only think of our up-coming wedding, with the knowledge that in six months I would finally be always with the woman that I so deeply loved. I had never been in love before, and had never felt this way about anyone. Adriana was and still is so special to me.

As the bus driver was closing the lower storage compartment door, I looked out the window and saw Adriana. It seemed that she decided to come back anyway and see me off. One of Adriana's most endearing qualities is her stubbornness. If she really wants to do something, she will do it no matter what anyone says or thinks. She stood on the platform blowing me kisses and waving. Looking down at her with a big smile, I waved and returned her kisses, as the bus driver closed the lower compartment door, took his seat and shifted the bus into gear. As the bus moved out into the street, Adriana walked along side of it waving at me, and actually followed the bus right onto the road, as it slowly merged into traffic. I watched with amazement as Adriana continued to move along side the bus waving. Looking out the window somewhat puzzled I was thinking to myself, "What are you doing?" As I looked closer, I noticed that she had a somewhat distressed look on her face as she dropped her wilted rose on the pavement and began to almost frantically wave her arms, when I realized all of a sudden, "Oh my God, her jacket is caught in the undercarriage door compartment." In a panic, with my breath trapped in my throat, I barely got two words out of my mouth when the bus driver noticed her dilemma in the side mirror and slammed on the breaks. The sudden stop of the bus, even though it was only crawling along, was enough to tear Adriana's jacket from the compartment door, as she fell to the pavement. On the heals of the bus driver, I ran out the door. One of us on each side of Adriana, we helped her to her feet. The bus driver was in a panic with a certain level of desperation in his voice, his face turning red and his eyes almost popping out of his head. He turned to me, firmly grabbing me with both hands on my left arm and staring into my eyes said, "Do you think Nancy knows that this is just a fictional prank?" Got yah! Although, I remember thinking at the time, I hope not, as I was planning on keeping my lovely editor going for a while yet. At any rate the cat is out of the bag, and all that is really left to do now is to delete this entire paragraph from the book, since it is made up and did not really happen. Okay Nancy, here is what you need to do, delete this paragraph starting with the sentence, "As the bus driver was closing the lower storage compartment door, I looked out the window and saw Adriana. It seemed…." Yes Nancy, after all these years, I finally got you!